**W9-BVU-944**

THE TIME
IS FULFILLED

# THE TIME IS FULFILLED

*Five Aspects of the Fulfilment of the Old Testament in the New*

by

F. F. BRUCE

WILLIAM B. EERDMANS PUBLISHING COMPANY
GRAND RAPIDS, MICHIGAN

**Library of Congress Cataloging in Publication Data**

Bruce, Frederick Fyvie, 1910-
  The time is fulfilled.

  (The Moore College lectures; 1977)
  Includes index.
  1. Bible. N.T. — Relation to the Old Testament —
Addresses, essays, lectures. I. Title. II. Series:
Moore Theological College, Sydney. The Moore College
lectures; 1977.
BS2387.B795    225.6    78-7373
ISBN 0-8028-1756-4

*To*
*the Principal and Faculty*
*Moore Theological College*
*Sydney,* N.S.W.

# CONTENTS

# LIST OF ABBREVIATIONS

| | |
|---|---|
| AV | Authorized (King James) Version |
| *BJRL* | *Bulletin of the John Rylands Library of Manchester* |
| CD | Book of the Covenant of Damascus |
| E.T. | English translation |
| *Hist. Eccl.* | *Ecclesiastical History* (Eusebius) |
| NEB | New English Bible |
| *NTS* | *New Testament Studies* |
| 1QM | War (*Milḥamah*) Scroll from Qumran Cave 1 |
| 1QS | Rule (*Serek*) of the Community from Qumran Cave 1 |
| 1QSa | Rule (*Serek*) of the Congregation from Qumran Cave 1 |
| RSV | Revised Standard Version |
| *SJT* | *Scottish Journal of Theology* |
| TB | Babylonian Talmud |
| *TDNT* | *Theological Dictionary of the New Testament*, E. T. (Grand Rapids, 1964–76) |
| TJ | Jerusalem (Palestinian) Talmud |

# PREFACE

When I was honoured with the invitation to deliver the inaugural series of annual Moore College Lectures in Sydney, N.S.W., it was suggested to me that some treatment of the fulfilment of the Old Testament in the New would be an acceptable subject; and I gladly agreed to this. The subject was one to which I had devoted some attention in previous lectures and publications, but there were many aspects of it which I had not touched upon, and of these further aspects I have chosen for the present series five which seem to me to be of considerable importance.

The five lectures were delivered in the earlier part of September 1977, and in presenting them now in print I recall gratefully the kindness shown me by many Australian friends during that visit, not least by my old friend Dr D. Broughton Knox, Principal of Moore Theological College, and by my former student Dr P. T. O'Brien, secretary of the Moore College Lectureship.

To Miss Margaret Hogg my best thanks are due for her careful typing of the manuscript.

*March 1978*                                          F. F. B.

# CHAPTER I

# THE TIME IS FULFILLED

*(Mark 1: 15)*

# THE TIME IS FULFILLED

*(Mark 1: 15)*

According to Mark's record, Jesus began his Galilaean ministry after John the Baptist was "delivered up", and the burden of his preaching was: "The time is fulfilled, and the kingdom of God has drawn near; repent, and believe in the good news" (Mark 1: 14 f.).

## 1. The note of fulfilment

These words express, among other things, the assurance that an ardently desired new order, long since foretold and awaited, was now on the point of realization. We today understand something of the nature of this new order because Jesus' announcement is read by us in the light of the fuller account of his ministry of word and action, temptation and passion, which it introduces. In a different context the same announcement could bear quite another meaning. Judas the Galilaean a generation earlier, and the Zealots who fanned the revolt against Rome a generation later, might well have announced their programmes in very similar terms.

Judas the Galilaean, according to Josephus, proclaimed a

new "philosophy"[1] – something that no previous religious teacher in Israel had proclaimed. He insisted that it was impermissible for the people of God, living in his land, to pay a pagan overlord tribute exacted on themselves (*tributum capitis*) or on the land (*tributum soli*). But in earlier days, when Assyrian or Babylonian conquerors imposed tribute on Israel or Judah, the prophets taught that their imposition of such tribute must be accepted as a divine judgment on the people for unfaithfulness; and when, after the return from exile, the Persian kings and their successors exacted tribute, the tribute seems to have been regarded as a price well worth paying for the peace and religious freedom which the imperial power safeguarded.

Why did Judas not take the same line? Because, according to Josephus, he and his adherents had "an unshakeable passion for liberty, having come to the conviction that God is the only governor and lord".[2] This may be interpreted to mean that, in Judas's view, a new order had been (or was about to be) introduced which was marked in a special and unprecedented manner by the kingship of God. The question should be carefully considered if Judas had reached the conclusion that the time had come, as foretold in the book of Daniel, for the God of heaven to set up a kingdom which would never be destroyed but would endure for ever.[3] The setting up of this kingdom meant the supersession of Gentile world dominion; therefore, whatever validity such dominion might have had in earlier days had now come to an end. For the holy people of the Most High, who under God were to exercise authority in this new and eternal kingdom, to continue to acknowledge pagan rulers or pay them tribute was a

1. *Antiquities* xviii. 4 ff.; cf. his *Jewish War* ii. 118.
2. *Antiquities* xviii. 23.
3. Dan. 2: 44; 7: 14, 27.

contradiction in terms, if it was not indeed high treason against Israel's true and only king.

So Judas's new "philosophy" may be understood. The situation becomes clearer sixty years later, when the thinking behind the revolt of A.D. 66 is said, by both Jewish and Roman writers, to have been stimulated by an oracle in the Jews' sacred writings which foretold that at that very time world dominion would fall to a man or men from Judaea. Josephus, Tacitus and Suetonius all take this oracle seriously, but indicate that it really pointed to Vespasian,[4] commander-in-chief of the Roman forces in Judaea charged with the suppression of the revolt, who with his sons Titus and Domitian acceded to the imperial power.

We may be sure that, whatever the oracle meant, it did not point to the Flavian emperors – but what *was* this oracle? We might think of Jacob's blessing of Judah in Genesis 49: 10:

> The sceptre shall not depart from Judah,
>     nor the ruler's staff from between his feet,
> until he comes to whom it belongs,
>     and to him shall be the obedience of the peoples.

The "sceptre" of this prophecy was identified in some quarters (as in the Qumran community)[5] with the "sceptre" in that oracle of Balaam (Num. 24: 17) which foretells how

> a star shall come forth out of Jacob,
>     and a sceptre shall rise out of Israel –

words which, as we know, were associated with the overthrow of Gentile overlords from the Qumran *Rule of War*[6] to

---

4. Josephus, *Jewish War* vi. 312 f.; Tacitus, *Histories* v. 13; Suetonius, *Vespasian* 4.
5. CD 7: 19 f.
6. 1 QM 11: 6.

the Bar-kokhba revolt of A.D. 132–135.[7] They are perhaps
not so apposite to the situation with which we are concerned
as is Jacob's blessing of Judah, since they make no explicit
reference to Judaea.

But what is the relevance to either of these oracles of the
emphatic indication that the dominion of which they spoke
was to be manifested *at that very time*? Oracles which appear to
specify the time of their fulfilment with any precision are not
common in the Old Testament, but Josephus notes one
exception: Daniel, he says, in common with other prophets,
foretold future events but, unlike them, he also foretold the
fixed time at which they would take place.[8] (In Daniel, it
might be said, were conjoined the two forms of divine com-
munication which, according to the exegetical principles of
the Qumran community, were usually separate: God gave
the prophets knowledge of what he was going to do, but
withheld from them knowledge of the time at which he was
going to do it; it was the impartation of this last knowledge to
the Teacher of Righteousness that put into his hand the key
to unlock the meaning of the prophecies.)[9]

When Josephus appeals to Daniel's visions as evidence
that God has a concern for human affairs and reveals to his
servants not only *what* must come to pass but *when* it will
come to pass, he may well have had in mind the prophetic
gift which he claimed for himself, which enabled him to
discern in Vespasian the predicted ruler of earlier oracles
and the coming prince of Daniel's oracle of the seventy heptads.[10] Perhaps Josephus honestly, but mistakenly, thought
that the "anointed prince" of Daniel 9: 25 (a Jewish leader)

7. Simeon ben Kosebah received the sobriquet Bar-kokhba ("son of the star")
from Rabbi Aqiba, who hailed him as the promised "star out of Jacob" (TJ *Ta'anit*
iv. 5 f., 21a, tr. M. Schwab, vi [Paris, 1883], p. 189).

8. *Antiquities* x. 267, 277 ff.

9. Cf. F. F. Bruce, *Biblical Exegesis in the Qumran Texts* (London, 1960), pp. 7 ff.

10. *Jewish War* iii. 351 ff.

and the "coming prince" of verse 26 (a destroyer of the holy city and sanctuary) were one and the same personage (whom he identified with Vespasian); what is more important is that both he and other Jews reckoned that Daniel's seventy heptads were on the point of being fulfilled. He deplores the misguided interpretation put upon the oracle by those Jews who found in it their "chief inducement to go to war" because they took it to portend the triumph of their own race.[11]

An investigation of the interpretations – or reinterpretations – of Daniel's oracle of the seventy heptads just before and during the first century A.D. would be a rewarding research project. The traditional Jewish chronology set out in the tractate *Seder 'Olam* (the chronology according to which the years from the creation of the world are still reckoned in the official Jewish calendar, so that Anno Mundi 5738 begins on September 13, 1977) is one surviving example of the interpretation which makes the seventy heptads expire with the Romans' destruction of the city and temple of Jerusalem.[12] But such a research project would make only a marginal contribution to the understanding of the New Testament. The influence of the book of Daniel on the New Testament is deep and pervasive, but the calculation of the seventy heptads has made little impression on it.[13]

## 2. The message of the kingdom

When Jesus proclaimed "The time is fulfilled", it is

---

11. *Jewish War* vi. 312.

12. This scheme makes the seventy heptads stretch from the destruction of the first temple by the Babylonians to the destruction of the second temple by the Romans, and thus shortens the actual length of the interval by 166 years.

13. The only direct New Testament echo of the calculation is the repeated reference to three and a half years (or 42 months or 1260 days) in the Apocalypse (Rev. 11: 2 f.; 12: 6; 13: 5); cf. the half-week of Daniel 9: 27.

improbable (to put it mildly) that he meant that the full tale
of the seventy heptads had now come to an end. Some of his
hearers may have understood him in this sense, but there is
no evidence that they did so. There are nevertheless unmis-
takable echoes of the book of Daniel in the form and content
of his proclamation, and in the eschatological sensitivity of
the situation in which he made it many of his hearers must
have been aware of these echoes. For example, his
announcement, "The time is fulfilled and the kingdom of
God has drawn near", may well have reminded some of them
of the words of Daniel 7: 22, "the time came for the saints to
receive the kingdom". But whether it reminded them of that
precise text or not, the general implication of the announcement was plain: the time had come when the God of heaven
was to inaugurate the indestructible kingdom which would
supersede all other forms of world dominion. The difference
between his announcement and an announcement such as
Judas the Galilaean and his spiritual heirs might have made
in similar terms lay in the difference between Jesus' conception of the kingdom of God and theirs, and this difference
reflected ultimately the difference between Jesus' conception
of God and theirs.

When the imprisoned John the Baptist sent his messengers to ask Jesus if he was the Coming One after all, or if they
had to look for someone else, he was perhaps disturbed by
the discrepancy between the purifying judgment by wind
and fire which he had said the Coming One would execute
and the ministry in which Jesus was actually engaged. When
Jesus told John's messengers to go back and tell their teacher
what they had seen him do and heard him say – "the blind
receive their sight, the lame walk, lepers are cleansed, and
the deaf hear, the dead are raised up, the poor have good
news preached to them" (Luke 7: 22) – he knew that John
would recognize the fulfilment of those prophetic words of

Isa. 35: 5 f. and similar scriptures which foretell how on the day of Yahweh's saving action

> the eyes of the blind shall be opened,
>   and the ears of the deaf unstopped;
> then shall the lame man leap like a hart
>   and the tongue of the dumb sing for joy.

Above all, the proclamation of the good news to the poor or afflicted was a sign that the year of Yahweh's favour had come, according to the announcement of the Spirit-anointed speaker of Isa. 61: 1 f., which (as we are told in Luke 4: 17–19) Jesus chose as his text and applied to his ministry in his programmatic sermon in the synagogue of Nazareth. No wonder, then that John was encouraged with the blessing invoked by Jesus on the one who refused to think that Jesus had let him down: Jesus was indeed the Coming One.

The enemy which Jesus confronted and challenged in his ministry was not the Roman oppressor but the spiritual power of darkness, the dominion of Satan. "If I by the finger of God cast out demons", he said, "then the kingdom of God has come upon you" (Luke 11: 20). The proclamation of the advent of the divine kingdom stirred up specially hostile activity in the realm of evil, which felt its dominion threatened. The superior power of the kingdom of God was seen in the release of those whose minds and bodies were held in spiritual bondage: Jesus not only proclaimed but effected "liberty to the captives and release to the enchained" (Isa. 61: 1). In doing so he knew himself to be the agent of the Father who desired the well-being, not the suffering, of his children.

When Jesus spoke of God as Father, or spoke *to* him as Father, he used the designation *Abba* rather than the liturgical *'abînû* ("our Father") by which God was addressed in

certain synagogue prayers or even the more personal 'abî
("my Father"). In calling God *Abba* – the domestic word by
which a father was known in the affectionate intimacy of the
family circle – Jesus appears to have been unique.[14] By
means of this word he expressed his own sense of loving
nearness to God and his own implicit trust in him, and he
taught his disciples to use it too and look to God with the
same trustful expectancy as children show when they look to
their fathers to provide them with food and clothes. Such an
attitude to God is of the essence of the kingdom of God; it
finds expression, for example, in the Lord's Prayer where the
disciples were taught to pray almost in the same breath for
the accomplishment of God's purpose in the world and for
their daily bread, the forgiveness of their sins, and deliverance in the hour of trial. So distinctive a locution of Jesus and
(following him) of his disciples was *Abba* that later the word
passed unchanged into the vocabulary of Gentile Christians:
Paul, for instance, assumes that it is as familiar to the Roman
Christians, whom he did not know personally, as it was to the
Galatian Christians, who were his own converts and presumably learned the usage from Paul himself (Rom. 8: 15;
Gal. 4: 6).

Those who render allegiance to the kingdom of God, the
disciples of Jesus, are true children of this heavenly Father,
and manifest this by reproducing his character. As he is
all-embracing in his goodness, so must they be: "Be merciful,
even as your Father is merciful" (Luke 6: 36). There was
nothing essentially new in this: one section of Leviticus is
known as the "law of holiness" because of its insistence on
the principle: "I am Yahweh your God . . .; be holy, for I am
holy" (Lev. 11: 44, etc.). In the same spirit one of the
Aramaic targums on Lev. 22: 28 (a passage enjoining

14. Cf. J. Jeremias, *The Central Message of the New Testament* (London, 1965), pp.
9 ff.; *Abba* (Göttingen, 1966), pp. 15 ff.

humane treatment of animals) says: "As our Father is merciful in heaven, so you must be merciful on earth".[15] But this note receives a central emphasis in Jesus' teaching about the kingdom of God which gives character to the whole.

The same lesson is driven home in a variety of parables illustrating different aspects of the kindness and forgiving love of God. Those in whose lives such qualities are manifested are pronounced happy; they are the people who are really to be congratulated, not the self-assertive pushers. Jesus' injunctions to his disciples not to meet oppression with violent resistance but to repay evil with good were a far cry from the policy of Judas the Galilaean and his followers. The latter used their oppressors' weapons and attacked brute force with brute force; the way of Jesus was actually a much more revolutionary course, and in the end it was to the way of Jesus, not of Judas, that the Roman Empire capitulated.

By such teaching, together with the active ministry which accompanied it, Jesus showed the character of the kingdom which he proclaimed. But while his works of mercy and power signified the presence of that kingdom, he made it plain that the hope of the ages was not yet consummated. During his ministry the kingdom of God was in course of inauguration; one day, within the lifetime of some of his hearers, it would come "with power" (Mark 9: 1). The powers of the kingdom of God were already at work, yet his disciples were encouraged to pray that the kingdom might come. But the consummated kingdom would bear the same character as the kingdom which was even now breaking in. Some of his disciples imagined that when it was finally established they would be compensated by positions of authority for the privations and dangers which they were currently enduring for its sake. On the contrary, said Jesus,

15. This paraphrase from the Pseudo-Jonathan Targum appears to have become a well-known quotation: it is cited more than once in the Palestinian Talmud.

the way to honour in the kingdom of God was the way of
service: the honour was not the *compensation* for the service;
the service *was* the honour. And he himself set them an
example, coming as he did not to receive service but to give it
and to crown that service by giving his life for others (cf.
Mark 10: 35–45).[16] In Origen's great word Jesus was the
*autobasileia*, the kingdom in person;[17] for never was the way of
the kingdom more fully seen than in him who said to his
Father, "Not my will, but thine, be done" (Mark 14: 36), and
accepted the cross in that spirit.

Jesus appears to have envisaged his sacrifice and death as
the means by which the limitations at present impeding the
progress of the kingdom would be removed. "I have a baptism to undergo", he said, "and how hampered I am until
the ordeal is past!" (Luke 12: 50). But his death would
unleash the powers of the kingdom of God and lead to the
bestowal of blessing and liberation on a far wider scale than
had thus far been possible.

However Jesus may have envisaged the coming of the
kingdom "with power", the early Christians appear to have
associated it with his resurrection. Paul speaks of him as
having been appointed Son of God "with power" by the
resurrection (Rom. 1: 4). To Paul's way of thinking, Jesus
had never been anything other than the Son of God, but
whereas, during his ministry and especially in his death, he
was the Son of God "in weakness", in resurrection he was
alive "by the power of God" (2 Cor. 13: 4).

### 3. The Son of Man

Jesus knew himself to be the Son of God, and that in no
merely official or formal sense: he was intensely aware of a

16. See p. 29.
17. Origen, *Commentary on Matthew*, 14: 7 (on Matt. 18: 23).

constant and peculiarly intimate filial relationship to God. But he did not usually speak of himself in public as the Son of God; his preferred self-designation was "the Son of Man". When he stood before the Sanhedrin and the high priest asked him point-blank if he was the Messiah, the Son of the Blessed One, he replied in terms which probably meant, "If that is the language which you insist on using, then my answer must be 'Yes'; but if I may choose my own language, this is what I say: 'You shall see the Son of Man seated at the right hand of the Almighty and coming with the clouds of heaven' " (Mark 14: 62).

This is the last recorded occasion on which he used the designation "the Son of Man", and the context with which he supplied it indicates its source. In the vision in which Daniel foresaw the time when the saints of the Most High would receive the kingdom, the saints were associated, if not identified, with "one like a son of man", a man-like figure, who came with the clouds of heaven into the presence of the eternal God, "the Ancient of Days", to receive from him the world dominion which had hitherto been wielded by pagan empires, portrayed as wild beasts. To the "one like a son of man" in the vision correspond "the saints of the Most High" in the angelic interpretation (Dan 7: 13 f., 18, 27). Jesus appears to have identified his followers with "the saints of the Most High", as when he said to them, "Fear not, little flock; for it is your Father's good pleasure to give you the kingdom" (Luke 12: 32). He spoke of himself as "the Son of Man" in the sense of "that (one like a) son of man" who receives the kingdom in Daniel's vision,[18] and promised them that they would share that kingdom with him if they were prepared to drink his cup and be baptized with his baptism (Mark 10: 38) – that is, share his suffering.

18. Cf. C. F. D. Moule, *The Origin of Christology* (Cambridge, 1977), pp. 11 ff.

But why should the Son of Man attain the kingdom through suffering – or, to put the question in Jesus' own words, "how is it written concerning the Son of Man that he should suffer many things and be treated with contempt?" (Mark 9: 12). It is true that, while suffering is not explicitly predicated of the "one like a son of man" in Daniel's vision, the saints of the Most High whom he represents are assailed and, for a time, overcome by the persecuting monarch depicted as the "little horn". Yet in the gospel record there is such repeated insistence, from Caesarea Philippi onwards, on the destined suffering of the Son of Man, that something more than an inference, however valid, from the oppression of the saints of the Most High is required to explain it. That Jesus regarded the "necessity" of the Son of Man's suffering as something "written" concerning him is plain. "The Son of Man", he said at the Last Supper, "goes as it is written of him" (Mark 14: 21), and he submitted to his captors in Gethsemane with the words, "Let the scriptures be fulfilled" (Mark 14: 49). And while this evidence is derived predominantly from the Gospel of Mark, it is not confined to it. In a patently non-Markan passage in Luke, where Jesus speaks of the coming day of the Son of Man's manifestation, he adds, "But first he must suffer many things, and be rejected by this generation" (Luke 17: 25). (If it be suspected that this is a Markan insertion into a non-Markan context, let some material evidence for such a suggestion be produced.) Nor should we overlook the independent Johannine tradition, in its distinctive idiom, emphasizing that "the Son of Man must be lifted up" (John 3: 14; 8: 28; 12: 34) – an expression in which his suffering and glory are combined.

While Jesus no doubt had Daniel's vision originally in mind when he spoke of the Son of Man, the designation was sufficiently flexible for him to give it what meaning he chose. There is no evidence that between Daniel's time and his own anyone used the expression "the Son of Man" to denote a figure of the future. (There is, of course, the Son of Man in the *Similitudes of Enoch*, but the *Similitudes* are probably later than the other Enoch documents with which they have been transmitted, and may even – for aught we know to the contrary – be later than Jesus' time, although it is unnecessary to go so far as Dr J. T. Milik and date them in the third century A.D.)[19] Had Jesus spoken of the Messiah, for example, he would have conjured up in his hearers' minds a variety of (possibly conflicting) pictures, none of which would have corresponded to his intention. But when he spoke of the Son of Man, their response was rather "Who is this Son of Man?"[20] – and the answer to that question could be found only in what he said about the Son of Man.

One of the most curious phenomena of some Gospel criticism is an unwillingness to allow that Jesus spoke of the Son of Man, and especially that he spoke of himself as the Son of Man.[21] It is the more curious because those who insist on applying the most stringent criteria of authenticity to sayings ascribed to Jesus in the Gospels appeal first among these to the criterion of dissimilarity,[22] which ought to be a powerful argument for the authenticity of the designation "the Son of Man". According to this criterion, we can be reasonably sure of the authenticity of any saying ascribed to Jesus if it is unparalleled both in Jewish records and in the usage of the early church. The application of this criterion lies wide open

---

19. Cf. J. T. Milik, *The Books of Enoch* (Oxford, 1976), pp. 95 f.
20. Cf. John 12: 34.
21. Cf. H. B. Sharman, *Son of Man and Kingdom of God* (New York, 1943); P. Vielhauer, "Gottesreich und Menschensohn in der Verkündigung Jesu", *Festschrift für Günther Dehn* (Neukirchen, 1957), pp. 51 ff. N. Perrin, *Rediscovering the Teaching of Jesus* (London, 1967), p. 198, appears to conclude "that Jesus could not have spoken of the coming of the Son of man" because such a title did not exist in contemporary Judaism. That, in my judgment, is precisely why he did so speak.
22. For these criteria cf. N. Perrin, *Rediscovering the Teaching of Jesus*, pp. 39 ff.

to certain logical objections, but let that be for the present.[23] Here, on the lips of Jesus, we have this repeated locution, unparalleled in Judaism, while its use on the lips of Stephen (Acts 7: 56) is the exception that proves the rule so far as the early church is concerned.[24]

When Jesus is recorded as speaking of the Son of Man's coming in glory (Mark 8: 38; 13: 26), it is easy to link that with Daniel's vision. But his emphasis on the Son of Man's destined suffering is best understood if in his mind he fused the Danielic figure of "one like a son of man" with the Isaianic Servant of Yahweh who does expressly suffer many things and is despised and rejected by men.[25] It is not so fashionable nowadays to hold this view as it was thirty or forty years ago, but I remain persuaded that my Manchester predecessor, T. W. Manson, was right not only in holding this view but also in insisting on a corporate dimension to Jesus' understanding of the Son of Man.[26] Jesus encouraged his disciples to follow the way of the Son of Man, to take up their cross and go after him, to drink his cup and share his baptism. In the event, indeed, he took up the cross for himself, drained the bitter cup and endured the baptism alone; but when in resurrection he re-gathered his scattered flock it was to lay the same charge upon them once more, with greater assurance of their fulfilling it this time. Simon Peter, who had first heard the call "Follow me" by the Galilaean lake, heard it there again, and this time there was

23. Cf. M. D. Hooker, "On Using the Wrong Tool", *Theology* 75 (1972), pp. 570 ff.

24. Its use on Stephen's lips may imply that he was at that moment experiencing the fulfilment of the promise of Luke 12: 8. Its similar use on the lips of James the Just (Eusebius, *Hist. Eccl.* ii. 23. 13) is taken, with several other features, from the record of Stephen's martyrdom.

25. There may also be an echo of "the stone which the builders rejected" in Psalm 118: 22.

26. T. W. Manson, *The Teaching of Jesus* (Cambridge, [2]1935), pp. 211 ff.

no turning back, no thoughtless over-confidence and no humiliating denial.

There are, in fact, some indications that Daniel's "one like a son of man", with his associates, was identified from the first – i.e. by the seer himself – with the Isaianic Servant.[27] Among the associates of the man-like figure, the saints of the Most High, a place of distinction is given to "those who are wise among the people", the *maskilîm*, who bear the brunt of the persecution and by doing so procure deliverance for others as well as winning eternal glory for themselves. When the new age dawns it is the *maskilîm*, those who lead many to righteousness, who shine for ever like the stars of heaven (Dan. 12: 3). The verb of which *maskilîm* is a plural participle appears in another form, but in the same conjugation, in Isa. 52: 13, where Yahweh declares that his Servant will "deal wisely" (*yaskîl*); and if this is said of him at the beginning of the fourth Servant Song he is described towards the end as "making the many to be accounted righteous" (Isa. 53: 11).

In addition to the repeated statements that the Son of Man must suffer, Mark reports one saying of Jesus which has been thought by many to have a specially close link with the fourth Servant Song. That is the saying, already referred to, which concludes the incident initiated by James and John's request for preferential treatment in the coming kingdom: "even the Son of Man", said Jesus, "did not come to be served but to be a servant, and to give his life a ransom for many" (Mark 10: 45).[28] The link with the fourth Servant Song has been exaggerated by those who have tried to find in this saying

---

27. Cf. M. Black, "Servant of the Lord and Son of Man", *SJT* 6 (1953), pp. 1 ff.; also "The Son of Man Problem in Recent Research and Debate", *BJRL* 45 (1962–63), pp. 305 ff.

28. An obituary tribute to Professor Norman Perrin relates how, when he was asked informally in a friend's house one evening, "Norman, just what do you really feel is the core of being a Christian?" he replied by quoting these words of our Lord (*Criterion* [University of Chicago Divinity School], 16 [Winter 1977], p. 10).

something approaching a translation of expressions occurring in the Song. On the other hand, the link has been minimized, if not altogether denied, by some exceptionally able scholars.[29] C. K. Barrett, for example, in a paper contributed to the memorial volume for T. W. Manson, found the antecedents of "giving one's life a ransom for many" in the martyrs of the Maccabaean struggle, who prayed that their suffering might be accepted by God as an atonement for their fellow-countrymen.[30] It might be added that the members of the Qumran community similarly believed that their devotion and privation would make an effective expiation for the land of Israel, polluted as it was by ungodly leaders.[31]

But there is no evidence that either Jesus or Mark knew the second and fourth books of Maccabees, recent Hellenistic productions as they were, while there is ample evidence that they both knew the Hebrew book of Isaiah. The atoning efficacy ascribed to the martyrdoms in the books of Maccabees might itself owe something to the portrayal of the Isaianic Servant, as the Qumran doctrine of expiation certainly does. In any case, since Jesus insisted that the sufferings of the Son of Man were "written" concerning him, it is highly probable that he also found the "ransom for many" in the prophetic scriptures – and where more certainly than in the picture of the Servant who makes his life a guilt-offering and thus "bears the sin of many" (Isa. 53: 10, 12)?[32]

It is pointed out that in Luke's counterpart to Mark 10: 45 – Jesus' words about the nature of true greatness and sovereignty addressed to the apostles in the upper room, where he was among them as "one who serves" (Luke 22: 27)

29. Cf. C. K. Barrett, "The Background of Mark 10: 45", in *New Testament Essays . . . in Memory of T. W. Manson*, ed. A. J. B. Higgins (Manchester, 1959), pp. 1 ff.; M. D. Hooker, *Jesus and the Servant* (London, 1959).

30. Cf. 2 Macc. 7: 37 f.; 4 Macc. 6: 27 ff.; 17: 22.

31. Cf. 1 QS 8: 6 f., 10; 1 Q Sa 1: 3.

32. Cf. J. Jeremias, "Das Lösegeld für Viele", *Judaica* 3 (1948), pp. 249 ff.

– there is no mention of ransom.[33] But Luke is not following Mark here and deliberately omitting the ransom clause; he is following a source of his own and conforming to the general outlook and style of his whole work.[34] What the other evangelists thought may be seen from (say) Matthew's addition of the phrase "for the forgiveness of sins" to the words of institution spoken over the cup at the Last Supper (Matt. 26: 28) or John's report of the Baptist's proclamation of "the Lamb of God, who takes away the sin of the world" (John 1: 29) and of Jesus' own promise that he would give his "flesh" – i.e. himself, his life – "for the life of the world" (John 6: 51).[35]

The redemptive understanding of the death of Christ is not peculiar to Mark among the evangelists, and when, elsewhere in the New Testament, we find the same essential understanding in such widely disparate documents as the letters of Paul and the book of the Revelation, the most adequate conclusion is that it goes back to Jesus himself. The teaching is his, if the varying formulation is theirs.

## 4. The Lord of time

When we speak of Jesus as coming when the time was fulfilled, we should not underestimate the degree to which he, by his ministry and sacrifice, made the time at which in fact he came the time of fulfilment. Paul's words, "when the time had fully come, God sent his Son" (Gal. 4: 4), have

33. R. Bultmann expressed the opinion that "at the end Luke 22: 27 is doubtless original over against Mark 10: 45, which has formed its conception of Jesus from the redemption theories of Hellenistic Christianity" (*The History of the Synoptic Tradition*, E. T. [Oxford, 1963], p. 144) – the statement in the last clause being without historical foundation.

34. The soteriological significance of the death of Christ is not emphasized in Luke's writings. Acts 20: 28 is no real exception, since that is part of a speech by Paul.

35. See p. 43.

sometimes been illustrated by the argument that the world
into which Jesus came was – politically, culturally and
religiously – ready for his coming. There is much truth in
this, but if the argument be pressed too far, it can become a
*petitio principii*. What Paul means is that, in the purpose of
God, the time for his people to leave the leading-strings of
their spiritual infancy had now arrived, and its arrival was
not only marked but given actuality by the coming of the
One in whom they were to attain their spiritual majority.
Jesus does not passively respond to the conditions which are
ripe for his appearance; he takes the initiative and inaugu-
rates, if he does not indeed create, the fulness of time which
he announces.

# IT IS THEY THAT BEAR WITNESS TO ME

*(John 5: 39)*

# IT IS THEY THAT BEAR WITNESS TO ME

*(John 5: 39)*

"You search the scriptures", says Jesus to the religious
leaders in Jerusalem who have found fault with him for
claiming to exercise the divinely-delegated functions of rais-
ing the dead and pronouncing judgment – "you search the
scriptures, because you think that in them you have eternal
life; and it is they that bear witness to me; yet you refuse to
come to me that you may have life" (John 5: 39 f.).

In the immediate context, Jesus invokes a wide variety of
witnesses to the authenticity of his claims: the testimony of
John (the Baptist), the testimony of the Father, the testimony of his own works, the testimony of scripture. The
testimony of scripture involves pre-eminently the testimony
of Moses: "If you believed Moses", Jesus goes on to say,
"you would believe me, for he wrote of me. But if you do not
believe his writings, how will you believe my words?" (John
5: 46 f.). In speaking thus Jesus confirms the testimony of
Philip to Nathanael: "We have found him of whom Moses in
the law and also the prophets wrote, Jesus of Nazareth, the
son of Joseph" (John 1: 45).

Can we ascertain from the wider context of the Fourth
Gospel something about the specific terms in which the
scriptures, and Moses in particular, bore witness to the
coming Christ? I believe we can, and would direct attention

primarily to the passage about the coming prophet in
Deuteronomy 18.

## 1. The prophet like Moses

Looking forward to the Israelites' settlement in the promised land, Moses tells them that when they wish to ascertain
the will of God, they must not have recourse to necromancy,
soothsaying or divination such as the Canaanites practised.
When God wished to reveal his will to them he would do so
through a prophet, as he did through Moses. "Yahweh your
God will raise up for you a prophet like me from among you,
from your brethren – him you shall heed" (Deut. 18: 15).
According to Moses in the plains of Moab, Yahweh had
announced that he would do this thing nearly forty years
before, "at Horeb, on the day of the assembly" (Deut. 18:
16). In the Massoretic text of the Pentateuch there is no word
of this earlier announcement, but the Samaritan edition, true
to its propensity for filling in parallels, inserts it between
verses 21 and 22 of Exodus 20.[1]

It might be supposed that the announcement was fulfilled
every time a prophet was sent to communicate God's will to
the people. However, even in Deuteronomy itself, and in the
historical corpus which it introduces, it is clearly indicated
that not every prophet was a prophet like Moses. In the short
obituary notice of Moses with which Deuteronomy ends, it is
said that "there has not risen a prophet since in Israel like
Moses, whom Yahweh knew face to face" (Deut. 34: 10).
Earlier in the Pentateuchal narrative a distinction is made by
Yahweh between an ordinary prophet, to whom he would
make himself known in a vision, or "speak with him in a
dream", and "my servant Moses". "With him", says God,

1. Between verses 21 and 22 of Exodus 20 the Samaritan Bible inserts the
Hebrew text of Deut. 5: 28b, 29; 18: 18–22; 5: 30 f.

"I speak mouth to mouth, clearly, and not in dark speech, and he beholds the form of the LORD" (Num. 12: 6–8). It was long before a prophet of this calibre arose again in Israel. How extensive a perspective is implied in the language of Deut. 34: 10, "there has not arisen a prophet *since* ... like Moses", may be disputed; it is plain, however, that while Joshua succeeded to Moses' leadership, he did not succeed to his prophetic office.

In the course of pre-exilic history, only two prophets appear who are comparable with Moses. These are Samuel and Elijah. To Samuel, acknowledged by all Israel as "a prophet of the LORD", "the LORD revealed himself ... at Shiloh by the word of the LORD" (1 Sam. 3: 20 f.), after a long period of spiritual drought when "the word of the LORD was rare" and "there was no frequent vision" (1 Sam. 3: 1). Samuel, moreover, assumed the national leadership at a time when Israel's continued existence as a people was in jeopardy and, under God, he ensured its survival. He performed priestly functions as well at a time when the family of Eli comprised only minors, not only sacrificing but (which was much more important) acting as a prevalent intercessor on Israel's behalf. Moses and Samuel are coupled together by Jeremiah as two men of God who, for all their righteousness and intercessory power, could not have availed to save apostate Jerusalem had they been resident there in its last days (Jer. 15: 1).

Elijah, hailed as "Israel's chariot and horsemen" (2 Kings 2: 12), stood foursquare and resolute in a time of national apostasy and was the principal agent through whom Yahweh turned the people's hearts back to himself. His altar and sacrifice on Mount Carmel reveal him as exercising priestly functions on a national scale,[2] and when he gives

2. He built an altar of "twelve stones, according to the number of the tribes of the sons of Jacob, to whom the word of the LORD came, saying, 'Israel shall be your

orders in Yahweh's name, they are carried out in face of the known wishes of the royal court.[3] Ahab may be king, but it is Elijah who, in the Hebrew historian's estimation, is the true leader of Israel in his day. When Moses and Elijah appeared together on the mount of transfiguration, Elijah was not an unworthy companion for Moses.[4]

If in the pre-exilic period Samuel and Elijah were recognized as prophets of Mosaic stature, the belief grew up in the post-exilic age that there would be only one prophet like Moses after Moses himself, and that his appearance would mark the end of the current age and the dawn of the new age. The cessation of the prophetic gift lent strength to this expectation. It was taken for granted that many questions of sacred procedure must remain unsolved until a prophet – who might well be *the* prophet of the end-time – arose to declare the will of God in regard to them. In 1 Maccabees 4: 46, for example, the stones of the great altar which had been polluted by the super-imposition of the idolatrous altar were dismantled at the time of the re-dedication of the temple and stored in a suitable place until a prophet would appear to say what should be done with them. Again, when a popular assembly after the winning of independence from the Seleucids had to make provision for the high-priesthood, it decreed that Simon should be "high priest for ever" (i.e. that the high-priesthood should pass from him to his descendants) "until a trustworthy prophet should arise" (1 Macc. 14: 41) – a prophet, that is to say, who could give clear guidance about the high-priestly line.[5]

The identification of the prophet like Moses with the

name' " (1 Kings 18: 31 f.).

3. E.g. in his command for the destruction of the prophets of Baal (1 Kings 18: 40).

4. Mark 9: 4 and parallels.

5. A similar function is ascribed in Neh. 7: 65 to "a priest with Urim and Thummim" who would settle disputes about priestly lineage.

prophet of the end-time is seen in its most radical form among the Samaritans. The Samaritans did not recognize a succession of prophets as the Jews did: God's last revelation of his will had been granted to Moses, and there would be no further revelation until the prophet like Moses arose. It is on the prophet like Moses that what is loosely called the Samaritans' "messianic hope" was fixed. They had nothing to do with the tribe of Judah or a prince of the house of David: they looked for the prophet whom they called the *Taheb*, the "restorer". When, therefore, the Samaritan woman in John 4: 19 perceived that Jesus was a prophet, she may have implied much more than a Jewish speaker would have meant by the same words.

In Jewish thought the expected prophet was not necessarily substituted for the royal Messiah: the two figures might stand alongside each other, and even be accompanied by a third. Thus the Rule of the Qumran community lays down regulations which are to be valid "until the rise of a prophet and of the Messiahs of Israel and Aaron".[6] This is commonly interpreted as alluding to the royal and priestly Messiahs who were expected to arise at the end-time in company with the prophet like Moses.

To the same effect the document called 4Q Testimonia brings together three Pentateuchal texts which were believed to point forward respectively to these three figures: the divine announcement about the prophet like Moses, Balaam's description of the star out of Jacob (Num. 24: 17) and part of Moses' blessing of the tribe of Levi (Deut. 33: 8 ff.). The announcement of the prophet like Moses is quoted not according to the Massoretic text but from the context in which it first appears in the Samaritan Bible – from Exodus 20.

6. 1 QS 9: 11.

When, according to John 1: 19 ff., a delegation from
Jerusalem interviewed John the Baptist and asked which
figure of prophetic expectation he claimed to be, he declined
to be identified with any of them. When he had denied that
he was the Messiah or the returning Elijah foretold in
Malachi 4: 4 ff., they said, "Are you the prophet?" John had
no need to say "Which prophet?" He knew that they meant
the prophet like Moses, so he answered "No".

John, by his own confession, was neither the Messiah nor
the prophet like Moses; Jesus was both, as the Fourth Gospel
makes plain – and more besides. So far as his being the
prophet like Moses is concerned, this is repeatedly a confession on the lips of those who saw and heard him, people
who were not gifted with penetration into the full truth of his
person and mission. The figure of the prophet like Moses is
far from giving an adequate account of him, but it is true so
far as it goes: the evangelist nowhere hints otherwise.

Other New Testament strata attest Jesus' identification
with the prophet like Moses: Peter's speech in the temple
court, for example (Acts 3: 22 f.), and Stephen's defence
before the Sanhedrin (Acts 7: 37); but of special importance
is the voice from heaven at Jesus' transfiguration: "This is
my beloved Son; listen to him" (Mark 9: 7). There is a
similarity between this wording and the heavenly voice at
the baptism, with which indeed its text has been variously
contaminated in the course of transmission; but the distinctive clause "listen to him" or "pay heed to him" is certainly
derived from Deut. 18: 15, and points to Jesus as the prophet
*par excellence* as well as God's beloved Son.

There are two specially important places in the Fourth
Gospel where Jesus is hailed as "the prophet". In John 6: 14,
after the feeding of the multitude,[7] the people who had seen

7. See p. 42.

this "sign" said, "This is indeed the prophet who is to come into the world!" In John 7: 40, after Jesus had stood in the temple court on the last day of the feast of tabernacles and invited those who were thirsty to come to him and receive "living water",[8] some of his hearers said, "This is really the prophet". On both occasions they meant "the prophet like Moses". A later rabbi is credited with the observation: "As the first redeemer caused manna to descend, . . . so will the last redeemer cause manna to descend. . . . As the first redeemer made a well to rise, . . . so will the last redeemer bring up water"[9] – the first redeemer being Moses and the last redeemer the Messiah, envisaged in his rôle as a second Moses, the prophet like Moses.

The analogy of the manna becomes explicit in the narrative of John 6; the analogy of the water from the rock remains implicit in the narrative of John 7, but, even if implicit, it is there. We shall return to this in a moment, but at present we should look at a variant reading at the end of John 7.

Jesus' activity in the temple court during the feast of tabernacles caused great disturbance among members of the Sanhedrin, some of whom were disposed to take pre-emptive action against him. Nicodemus reminded them that it was illegal to pass judgment on a man without first hearing the evidence and giving him an opportunity to speak for himself. This provoked the scornful rejoinder, "Are you a Galilaean too? Search, and see that a prophet does not arise from Galilee" (John 7: 52). This was a curious statement: some of the prophets did probably arise from Galilee. But one witness to the text – papyrus 66, dated towards the end of the second century – makes the speakers say, "*the* prophet does not arise from Galilee". We have to bear in mind that this is very much a minority reading (albeit the reading of our

8. See p. 46.
9. *Ecclesiastes Rabba* on Eccles. 1: 9.

oldest witness to the text of this passage); nevertheless, it is
relevant in the context, and indeed heightens the Johannine
irony which infuses the context. Some said, "This is the
prophet"; others said, "This is the Messiah". To the latter
suggestion it is objected, "But the Messiah comes from
Bethlehem, not from Galilee". To the former suggestion it is
now objected, "But *the prophet* does not arise from Galilee".
How it could be known whence "the prophet" would arise is
not clear; the evangelist and his readers, however, know
something which enables them to savour the irony of the
situation: whether he was identified with the prophet or with
the Messiah, Jesus was born in Bethlehem, not in Galilee.

It is with special reference, however, to his function as the
spokesman of God, the prophet like Moses, that the scriptures, and especially the Pentateuchal scriptures, bear witness to him: "he whom God has sent utters the words of
God" (John 3: 34a).

## 2. The bread from heaven

The feeding of the five thousand, the only "sign" of the
Galilaean ministry common to the Fourth Gospel and the
other three, provides the cue in John's record for Jesus'
discourse on the bread of life, delivered in the Capernaum
synagogue. The discourse falls into three parts, with an
epilogue. Part 1 speaks of the true bread from heaven, of
which the manna eaten by the wilderness generation was but
a foreshadowing. The manna was God's gift, "the grain of
heaven" and "bread of the angels",[10] but those who ate it
*died* nonetheless. The true bread of God gives *life* to the
world: it bears the same relation to the manna as did the
living water of which Jesus spoke to the water in Jacob's well;

10. Psalm 78: 24 f.

and Jesus himself is the one authorized by God to impart the life-saving bread as he is the one who bestows the living water. As the Samaritan woman said "Sir, give me this water" (John 4: 15), so now Jesus' hearers say "Lord, give us this bread always" (John 6: 34).

This request leads on to Part 2 of the discourse: Jesus not only *gives* the bread of life; he *is* the bread of life: "he who comes to me will never hunger; he who believes on me will never thirst" (John 6: 38). Partaking of him who is the living bread means coming to him, believing in him. The result of so coming and believing is the possession of eternal life now and the certainty of resurrection at the last day (John 6: 40). The sacrificial implication of Jesus' claim to be the bread of life becomes explicit at the end of Part 2, "the bread which I shall give – for the life of the world – is my flesh" (John 6: 51).

This becomes the theme of Part 3: "unless you eat the flesh of the Son of Man and drink his blood, you have no life in you; it is he who eats my flesh and drinks my blood who has eternal life, and I will raise him up at the last day" (John 6: 53 f.). Faith in Christ is not simply a matter of accepting the gift he bestows: it involves appropriating him, partaking of him, union with him – "he who eats my flesh and drinks my blood abides in me and I in him" (John 6: 56).

The language is startling, not to say scandalous; but the impossibility of taking it literally challenges the hearer (or reader) to consider what it means. When Jesus says, "It is the Spirit that gives life; the flesh is of no avail" (John 6: 63), he shows that the eating and drinking of which he speaks denote an activity of the spiritual realm. Material food cannot impart spiritual life. The distinction between spirit and flesh here is as sharp as in the conversation with Nicodemus in chapter 3.

This part of the Capernaum discourse does not refer directly to the Eucharist, but it does expound in one way the

truth which the Eucharist sets forth in another – the truth
well summarized in the exhortation to the communicant in
the Book of Common Prayer: "Take and eat this in remem-
brance that Christ died for thee, and feed on him in thy heart
by faith with thanksgiving".

Thus, then, the Old Testament narrative of the manna is
interpreted so as to bear witness to Christ.


### 3. *The living water*

While Jesus both gives and is the bread of life, he does not
identify himself in this way with the living water which he
imparts. The evangelist sees in Jesus' words about the living
water a reference rather to the Spirit.

There are two places in the Fourth Gospel where the
theme of living water comes to the fore – the conversation at
Sychar's well and the proclamation in the temple court on
the last day of the Feast of Tabernacles.

The nature of the water which Jesus undertakes to give in
his conversation with the Samaritan woman is not expressly
specified, but can be plainly inferred nevertheless from his
words: "the water that I give him shall be in him a well of
water springing up unto life eternal" (John 4: 14). Of this
utterance, as of his later proclamation in the temple court,
the evangelist might well have said, "This he spoke of the
Spirit".[11]

The rabbis – or some of them – used similar language
regarding the Torah: of him "who labours in the Torah for
its own sake" Rabbi Meir said: "he is made like a never-
failing fountain and like a river that flows on with ever-
sustained vigour".[12] The Samaritans as well as the Jews had
their interpretation of the Torah, symbolized here perhaps

11. John 7: 39 (see p. 47).
12. *Pirqê Abot* 6: 1.

by Jacob's well, for Samaritans as well as Jews called Jacob "our father". For John, as for Paul, the age of Torah was superseded by the age of the Spirit through the completion of Jesus' earthly ministry; and for John this is relevant to Samaritans as much as to Jews. During the age of Torah their varying interpretations kept them apart; in the age of the Spirit that barrier is removed. Formerly it was a matter of importance whether the God of Israel was worshipped on Zion or on Gerizim; now "the hour is coming; it is already present", when the Father's worship is tied to neither of these sacred hills: the true worshippers, whether Jews or Samaritans (or non-Israelites altogether), worship him "in spirit and in truth", and have fellowship one with another in such spiritual worship (John 4: 23 f.).

The offer of living water at the feast of tabernacles, the annual harvest-home, includes an Old Testament reference which has not been identified with certainty. It is generally agreed that the offer was made against the background of the ceremony of water-pouring which took place on each of the first seven mornings of the festival. According to the Mishnah tractate *Sukkah*:

> They used to fill a golden pitcher holding one and a half pints with water from Siloam. When they reached the water gate they blew three blasts on the trumpet (*shofar*). The priest on duty ascended the altar-ramp and turned to the right, where there were two silver funnels . . ., the funnel to the west for libations of water and that to the east for wine.[13]

Into the western funnel the water from Siloam was poured as a libation – partly as an act of thanksgiving for the rain of the past season, without which there would have been no crops

13. *Sukkah* 4: 9.

to harvest, and partly as an act of prayer for a similar blessing in the season to come.

It was on the morning of the eighth day, when the ceremony of water-pouring was not enacted, that Jesus issued his invitation. In the absence of the material water he offered spiritual water:

> He that is athirst, let him come to me;
> And let him drink who believes in me.

(If we punctuate thus we have a rhythmical couplet.)[14] Then follows the scriptural allusion: "As the scripture has said, out of his belly shall flow rivers of living water".

As it stands, the statement suggests that the believer is not only personally refreshed by living water but becomes a channel through which it flows into the lives of others. C. F. Burney pointed out over fifty years ago that the Aramaic words for "belly" and "fountain" have the same consonants, and envisaged an Aramaic original meaning "rivers shall flow forth from the fountain of living waters" – i.e. God himself (cf. Jer. 2: 13).[15] This hypothesis is attractive but unnecessary. If we retain the Greek wording and render "out of his inmost part will flow rivers of living water" we may find the Old Testament source in those prophecies which foretell a day when, as it is put in Zech. 14: 8, "living waters shall flow out from Jerusalem" – from under the threshold of the temple, says Ezekiel (47: 1), "from the house of the LORD", says Joel (3: 18). In another Johannine book of the New Testament this stream becomes "the river of the water

---

14. This punctuation is supported by early Western textual and exegetical evidence (cf. the line-division in both Greek and Latin texts of Codex D).

15. C. F. Burney, *The Aramaic Origin of the Fourth Gospel* (Oxford, 1922), pp. 109 ff. Aramaic *me'în* means "belly" and *ma'yān* (the word used by Rabbi Meir in the saying quoted above, p. 44) means "fountain" (the consonantal spelling of both is *m'yn*).

of life, bright as crystal, flowing from the throne of God and of the Lamb", which waters the new Jerusalem and spreads life and healing wherever it flows (Rev. 22: 1 f.).[16] Here plainly the river has become a pictorial symbol of the blessings of the gospel. Something to the same effect is present in Jesus' words about living water, spoken in the temple court, interpreted by the evangelist as a reference to the Spirit, which believers in Jesus were to receive when once he was "glorified" (John 7: 39) – that is, in the idiom of the Fourth Gospel, when once he had returned to the Father by way of the cross.

The mention of Siloam in the ceremony of the water-pouring reminds us of the reference to the pool in the narrative of the cure of the blind man in John 9: 7. Here, however, it is enlightenment rather than refreshment that is in view. During the feast of tabernacles "there was not a courtyard in Jerusalem that did not reflect the light of the Beth-ha-She'ubah"[17] ("the place of water-drawing", as in Isa. 12: 3). The light of the world as well as the water of life was symbolized by features of this festival. When Jesus bids the blind man wash the clay from his eyes in the pool of Siloam, the evangelist notes that the name (Shiloah in Isa. 8: 6) means "sent";[18] the deeper meaning is that spiritual enlightenment can come only from the one whom God has sent.

### 4. The passover lamb

Attempts have been made in several places in the Fourth Gospel to find references to the passover lamb, especially to the passover lamb as having found its antitype in Jesus. The

16. See p. 113.
17. *Sukkah* 5: 3. The verb "draw" in Isa. 12: 3 is *shā'ab* (from which *she'ūbāh* is derived).
18. From Heb. *shālaḥ* ("send").

Johannine chronology of the passion season has been understood in this sense, and perhaps rightly. But the only unambiguous allusion of this kind to the passover lamb comes at the end of the passion narrative, where the soldiers who broke the legs of the two men crucified with Jesus are said not to have broken his, because he was already dead: "these things [the non-breaking of Jesus' legs] took place in order that the scripture might be fulfilled, 'No bone of him shall be broken' " (John 19: 36).

I have called this allusion to the passover lamb unambiguous, but that statement may have been too unqualified. Some students of this Gospel have seen here a reference to Psalm 34: 20, where God is viewed as the deliverer of the righteous man who trusts in him: "He (God) keeps all his bones: not one of them is broken." If this scripture were in the evangelist's mind here, it would underline Jesus' righteousness, and the vindication of his trust in God, much in the spirit of Luke's rendering of the centurion's testimony at the cross: "Certainly this man was innocent" (Luke 23: 47). But in Psalm 34: 20 the divine guarding of the righteous man's bones is a vivid expression for the preservation of his life and his general well-being. Thus, while C. H. Dodd (for example) finds a reference to Psalm 34: 20 "more likely" than one to the paschal lamb in John 19: 36,[19] it seems to me more likely that the evangelist had in mind the literal prescription with regard to the paschal lamb: "you shall not break a bone of it" (Exod. 12: 46; cf. Num. 9: 12). Jesus, in his eyes, is the antitypical paschal lamb; here at least John is in agreement with Paul: "Christ our passover has been sacrificed for us" (1 Cor. 5: 7).

It is doubtful if the title "the Lamb of God", given twice to Jesus by John the Baptist in the Fourth Gospel (John 1: 29,

19. C. H. Dodd, *The Interpretation of the Fourth Gospel* (Cambridge, 1953), p. 428, n. 1.

36), has a paschal reference: the passover lamb was not generally regarded as a sin-offering, whereas the Lamb of God is said to take away the sin of the world. Probably no one Old Testament passage underlines the designation "the Lamb of God"; rather it sums up a number of Old Testament themes, of which the passover lamb is one[20] – others being the lamb of God's providing spoken of by Abraham (Gen. 22: 8)[21] and (more especially) the suffering Servant, led like a lamb to the slaughter and giving his life as a sin-offering (Isa. 53: 7, 10).[22]

## 5. The King of Israel

When Nathanael in John 1: 49 hails Jesus not only as the Son of God but also as the King of Israel, he strikes a note which is echoed later in the Gospel. The Old Testament prophecies of a coming king were understood in various ways in the first century A.D. There were the militant messianists like those who, after the feeding of the multitude, tried to compel Jesus to be their king (John 6: 15). But he was not prepared to be the kind of king they wanted, and they were not interested in the only kind of kingship to which he laid any claim.

In the "parable" of the good shepherd in John 10: 1–30 Jesus presented himself, to those who understood his language, as the true king of Israel. In ancient Israel, as elsewhere in the Near East, the king, whether divine or human, is frequently portrayed as a shepherd. "Give ear, O Shepherd of Israel," prays the psalmist, "thou who leadest Joseph like a flock!" (Psalm 80: 1). If he who is enthroned

20. It is probably the passover lamb that is in view in the simile of 1 Pet. 1: 19, "a lamb without blemish or spot" (cf. Exod. 12: 5).

21. See p. 64.

22. See p. 30.

upon the cherubim is the Shepherd of Israel, the same title is borne by his anointed king. Of the coming "ruler in Israel" foretold in Micah 5: 2, the prophet goes on to say, "he shall stand and feed his flock in the strength of the LORD" (Micah 5: 4).

In the shepherd discourse of Ezekiel 34 Yahweh speaks as Israel's divine shepherd who appoints under-shepherds to care for his flock and denounces them for their breach of trust. His sheep have been scattered because of those under-shepherds' carelessness, but he himself will seek them out and gather them together again, giving special tendance to the weak and wounded among them. "And I will set up over them", he says, "one shepherd, my servant David, and he shall feed them; he shall feed them and be their shepherd. And I Yahweh will be their God, and my servant David shall be prince among them" (Ezek. 34: 23 f.). In Ezekiel's day "my servant David" cannot be the historical David; he is the coming son of David under whom lasting peace and prosperity would be established.

So, in John 10, Jesus describes himself as the good shepherd who assembles his sheep from the fold of Israel and protects them with his life, bringing to join them "other sheep . . ., not of this fold", so that there might be "one flock, one shepherd" (John 10: 16). The close association between Yahweh and his servant David in Ezekiel 34 is reflected in the close association between Jesus and his Father in John 10. "My sheep hear my voice, and I know them, and they follow me; and I give them eternal life, and they shall never perish, and no one shall snatch them out of my hand. My Father, who has given them to me, is greater than all, and no one is able to snatch them out of the Father's hand. I and the Father are one" (John 10: 27–30).

The kingly rôle of Jesus is underlined in the Fourth Evangelist's account of his entry into Jerusalem. The crowds who cry Hosanna expressly acclaim him as the King of Israel, and in John 12: 15 the oracle of Zech. 9: 9 is quoted in an abbreviated form:

> Fear not, daughter of Zion;
> behold, your king is coming,
> sitting on an ass's colt!

The nature of Jesus' kingship is suggested partly by the context of the Gospel narrative (not least in his choosing an ass for a mount) and partly by the context of the Zechariah oracle, where Zion's king puts an end to war and establishes world-wide peace. But John brings out its nature most tellingly in his report of the interchange between Jesus and Pilate at the end of chapter 18. The charge on which Jesus was brought before Pilate was that he claimed to be king of the Jews: that was, indeed, the charge on which he was sentenced to death, as the inscription on the cross testified. The implication of the charge was that he aimed at being the kind of king he refused to be in Galilee – a king such as the militant messianists looked for. He emphasizes to Pilate that he is not that kind of king at all: his kingship is the kingship that is acknowledged by those who are on the side of truth, who love the truth. As C. H. Dodd used to point out, readers of John's Gospel towards the end of the first century might not be interested in who was or was not legitimate king of the Jews in A.D. 30, but concern for truth is a mark of serious minds in all ages, and for such Jesus' true kingship is of abiding relevance.[23] But historically it was as king of the Jews that Jesus was crucified. John draws special attention to the inscription proclaiming his kingship – to its trilingual presentation; to its publicity, there by the roadside, where

23. C. H. Dodd, *About the Gospels* (Cambridge, 1950), pp. 37 f.

many were coming and going to the city or from it; to the chief priests' protest against Pilate's choice of words, and to Pilate's conclusive "What I have written, I have written" (John 19: 22). There, beneath that inscription, Jesus committed his spirit to God, and there, to make sure he was dead, "one of the soldiers pierced his side with a spear" (John 19: 34). And in the piercing John recognizes the fulfilment of another element in the Old Testament portrayal of Israel's true king. "Another scripture says, 'They shall look on him whom they have pierced' " (John 19: 37).

The reference is to Zech. 12: 10, a passage the historical context of which is difficult – perhaps impossible – to establish. I have discussed its relevance to the passion narrative in some detail elsewhere.[24] Suffice it to say here that the pierced one of the prophecy is probably the king, Yahweh's representative, "devoting" himself for the well-being of his subjects. In the opinion of some, the reference is to a moment in the national liturgy, in which the king suffered for his people's deliverance; in any case, both in the Massoretic text and in the Hebrew text underlying the Septuagint translation (or rather mistranslation)[25] Yahweh is the speaker: it is he who says "they shall look on me whom they have pierced, and they shall mourn for him ...". The awkwardness of the transition from the first person to the third is dealt with skilfully in the New English Bible, which renders "They shall look on me, on him whom they have pierced" (treating this as a quotation from some source, in which the king figured as Yahweh's representative),[26] and goes on, "and they shall wail over him ...". The repeated references to "the house of David" in the immediate context confirm that the king is in view. The exegesis of Zech. 12: 10 is not our

24. Cf. F. F. Bruce, *This is That* (Exeter, 1968), pp. 101 ff.
25. The Septuagint version misreads Heb. *dāqar* ("pierce") as *rāqad* ("dance").
26. NEB puts these words between quotation-marks.

present concern, however; the point to emphasize is that John sees in the piercing of the king of the Jews the fulfilment of a royal oracle in which, as in Ezekiel's shepherd oracle, Yahweh and his anointed are one.

The shepherd-king is pierced, and from his piercing flows salvation for the world. This is the witness borne by the last prophetic *testimonium* cited in the Gospel of John; and on this particular witness John lays exceptional emphasis because it will help so greatly to promote the purpose of his Gospel – the awakening or strengthening of his readers' faith in Jesus as "the Christ, the Son of God" (John 20: 31). If, for him, the cross of Christ is the supreme unfolding of the incarnate glory, here he finds the inmost significance of that unfolding. What Mark teaches in one way by his record of the rent veil,[27] John teaches in another way by his record of the piercing; and to the testimony of the scriptures which he quotes he adds the testimony of an eyewitness: "He who saw it has borne witness – his testimony is true, and he knows that he tells the truth – that you also may believe" (John 19: 35).

27. Mark 15: 38.

# ABRAHAM OUR FATHER

*(Romans 4: 1)*

# ABRAHAM OUR FATHER

*(Romans 4: 1)*

When Paul affirms that the gospel of justification by faith, far from nullifying the Old Testament law, rather establishes it, he appeals in the first instance to the record of Abraham.

## 1. *In the Old Testament*

In the Old and New Testaments alike Abraham is the prototype of those who are elected by God.

It might be said, indeed, that Noah, not Abraham, was the first man in the biblical record to be chosen: although the actual word is not used of him, he (with his family) was certainly selected to live out of the *massa perditionis* of mankind in his day. But, if we grant this, we must make the point that, whereas the election of Noah and his family meant the destruction of the rest of mankind, the election of Abraham and his family meant the blessing of the rest of mankind; and it is Abraham's election, not Noah's, that provides the scriptural prototype for God's electing grace. As Abraham's election was designed to bring blessing to "all the families of the earth" (Gen. 12: 3), so Abraham's spiritual progeny, described in Eph. 1: 4 as "chosen in Christ before the world's foundation to be holy and blameless in the sight of God", are presented not only as God's masterpiece of reconciliation but also as his pilot scheme for the reconciled universe of the future. The same insight finds expression in the idiom of the Apocalypse, where the nations walk in the light of the new Jerusalem (Rev. 21: 24).

In the narrative of Genesis 12 ff., Abraham is called by God to leave his ancestral home for an unknown land which was to be the inheritance of himself and his descendants, and he received unprecedented promises, including the promise of such blessing from God that he and his family would become a proverbial standard for blessing, if not indeed a means of blessing, to all the families of earth. He responded obediently to the divine call and "went out, not knowing whither he went". His readiness to believe the divine promise, and live in the good of it, was the more remarkable because its fulfilment depended on his having a numerous posterity, and when the promise was given, he was childless and no longer young. Yet "he believed in the LORD, and he counted it to him for righteousness" (Gen. 15: 6).

His significance in the history of the people of God is summed up in the exordium of Ezra's prayer at the reading of the law: "Thou art Yahweh, the God who didst choose Abram and bring him forth out of Ur of the Chaldaeans and give him the name Abraham; and thou didst find his heart faithful before thee; and didst make with him the covenant to give to his descendants the land of the Canaanite . . .; and thou hast fulfilled thy promise, for thou art righteous" (Neh. 9: 7 f.).

Outside the patriarchal narrative of Genesis, Abraham does not figure frequently in the Old Testament – not so frequently, for example, as his grandson Jacob. But when he is mentioned, no doubt is left of his pre-eminence in salvation history or in popular memory. The people of Israel are the offspring of Abraham, "the people of the God of Abraham"

(Ps. 47: 9), and, above all, they are the heirs of the sworn promise, the covenant which God made with Abraham and reaffirmed with Isaac and Jacob. When they were oppressed in Egypt, God "remembered his covenant with Abraham, with Isaac and with Jacob", and "came down to deliver them" (Exod. 2: 24; 3: 8). When he threatened to wipe them out for their worship of the golden calf, Moses made effective intercession for them by reminding him of that covenant: "Remember Abraham, Isaac, and Israel, thy servants, to whom thou didst swear by thine own self, . . . 'all this land that I have promised I will give to your descendants, and they shall inherit it for ever' " (Exod. 32: 13). In later generations a psalmist could look back to Israel's wilderness wanderings and recall how God supplied them with "bread from heaven" and "water from the rock" because "he remembered his holy promise, and Abraham his servant" (Ps. 105: 40–42).

In days of declension, exile and restoration the memory of the covenant with Abraham was a basis for hope. The book of Micah ends with a triumphant celebration of the pardoning grace of Israel's incomparable God (Micah 7: 18–20):

> Thou wilt cast all our sins
>   into the depths of the sea.
> Thou wilt show faithfulness to Jacob
>   and steadfast love to Abraham,
> as thou hast sworn to our fathers
>   from the days of old.

The remnant that was left in Judaea by Nebuchadrezzar after the deportation of their fellow-countrymen comforted themselves with the reflexion that, if the land was promised to Abraham, one man though he was, they were certainly more numerous than he and would certainly possess the land

(Ezek. 33: 24). The exiles, they thought, would never be heard of again. But they were wrong. One prophet after another insisted that, in the mercy of God, the hope of the future lay with the exiles and not with "the people of the land".[1]

It was the returning exiles, "the offspring of Abraham my friend" (Isa. 41: 8), who received the divine exhortation (Isa. 51: 1 f.):

> Look to the rock from which you were hewn,
>     and the quarry from which you were digged;
> Look to Abraham your father
>     and to Sarah who bore you,
> for when he was but one I called him,
>     and I blessed him and made him many.

Here it is apposite to recall the late midrash which explained why Abraham was called "the rock" in these terms: "A certain king desired to build a palace, so his servants started digging to find a foundation. They dug for a long time and then for a long time again, but found nothing but morass. At last they struck solid rock and he said, 'Now I can begin to build'."[2] The appositeness of the midrash lies not only in its application to Abraham but also in the analogy it presents to the Matthaean logion: "On this rock I will build my church" (Matt. 16: 18).

It may be that in the situation after the return from exile there was a tendency for some groups to claim Abrahamic

---

1. Cf Jer. 24: 1–10; 29: 1–19.

2. Preserved in the mediaeval collection *Yalquṭ Shimeʿoni* (1: 766). A similar story appears in *Exodus Rabba* 15: 7 (on Exod. 12: 2) where, however, it is not Abraham in particular but the three patriarchs together that constitute the foundation rock. The two occasions on which (after long digging) soundings revealed nothing but morass correspond to the generation of Enosh and the generation of the flood. The word rendered "rock" in the midrash is *peṭra*, a loanword from Greek.

descent, or at least the Abrahamic heritage, exclusively for themselves. We may hear in Isa. 63: 16 the complaint of an excluded community as they say to the God of their fathers:

> Thou art our Father,
>> though Abraham does not know us
>> and Israel does not acknowledge us;
> thou, O LORD, art our Father,
>> our Redeemer from of old is thy name.

## 2. *In the gospel tradition*

As time went on, it was made increasingly clear that descent from Abraham was not everything, least of all for those who most confidently claimed it.

But few dismissed the idea of Abrahamic descent so sweepingly as John the Baptist, when he preached his message of repentance to the crowds that came to hear him in the Jordan valley: "Don't start to say to yourselves, 'We have Abraham as our father'; I tell you, God can raise up children to Abraham from the stones on the ground" (Matt. 3: 9; Luke 3: 8). Descent from Abraham carried with it no special privilege or merit (even vicarious merit), no special exemption from the wrath to come. If John's baptism was an extension of proselyte baptism to the chosen people,[3] then his baptism, like his preaching, meant that even the descendants of Abraham must take the outside place, like lesser breeds without the law, and enter the eschatological community, the people prepared for the Lord, by repentance and baptism just as Gentiles had to do when they became converts to the commonwealth of Israel.

3. Cf. H. H. Rowley, "Jewish Proselyte Baptism and the Baptism of John", *From Moses to Qumran* (London, 1963), pp. 211 ff.

There is nothing quite so radical as this in the teaching of Jesus recorded in the Synoptic Gospels, although he does warn his hearers, who were of course descended from Abraham and the other patriarchs, that some of them will have good cause to weep in frustration when they see Abraham, Isaac and Jacob and the prophets in the kingdom of God, together with many from east and west, while they themselves are excluded from the feast (Matt. 8: 11 f.; Luke 13: 28 f.). If the many from east and west who take the place of the excluded "sons of the kingdom" are Gentiles (as they apparently are in the Matthaean context, where Jesus praises the Capernaum centurion's faith), this comes very near to acknowledging Gentiles as in some sense children of Abraham, though this is not explicitly said.

A much less radical reference appears in the special Lukan material in the Third Gospel where Jesus defends his healing of a deformed woman in synagogue one sabbath day by asserting that that was the most appropriate of all days for setting "a daughter of Abraham" free from her "bond" (Luke 13: 16). Even so, there is an element of social radicalism here, characteristic of Jesus and particularly congenial to Luke, in that "a daughter of Abraham" (by natural descent, of course) is treated as having equal rights with any son of Abraham.

In the distinctive Lukan material Abraham appears in person in the parable of the rich man and Lazarus, where Lazarus reclines next to him in the other world, as the beloved disciple did to Jesus at the Last Supper according to John 13: 23–25. The rich man in Hades calls him "Father Abraham", and Abraham addresses him as "son" – but the relationship, though acknowledged on both sides, does the rich man no good. He had failed to recognize Lazarus as a fellow-member of the family of Abraham on earth, and now he was reaping what he had sown.

A similar moral is attached to the account of Jesus' interview with a rich man preserved by the uncanonical Gospel according to the Hebrews. When the rich man, like his canonical counterpart in Mark 10: 20, claims to have kept the commandments, "the Lord said to him: 'How can you say, "I have kept the law and the prophets"? It is written in the law: "You shall love your neighbour as yourself" – and look, many of your brothers, sons of Abraham, are dressed in filthy rags and are dying of hunger, while your house is full of many good things, yet nothing at all goes forth from it to them'." This account, indeed, amplifies the narrative of the rich ruler in Mark 10: 17–22 with elements from the Lukan parable of Dives and Lazarus.

In the Fourth Gospel there is a similar insistence that mere physical descent from Abraham is insufficient. To some Jews who entered into debate with him and claimed to be Abraham's descendants, Jesus replied that he acknowledged their descent from Abraham in a biological sense but denied it in the sense that really mattered: "If you were Abraham's children you would do what Abraham did" – but their attempt on his life pointed to a very different spiritual ancestry for them (John 8: 33–44).

As the dispute advanced, Jesus made the further statement, "Your father Abraham rejoiced that he was to see my day; he saw it and was glad" (John 8: 56). The statement puzzled his hearers, and no wonder: we ourselves are still not sure of its meaning. But one attractive possibility is that it refers to the "binding of Isaac" (as the incident of Gen. 22: 1–19 is called in Jewish tradition). In this connexion we may recall the passage in the *Testament of Levi* which speaks of the rise of a "new priest" (18: 1–6):

The heavens shall be opened
And out of the sanctuary of glory sanctification shall

come upon him
With a father's voice as from Abraham to Isaac.

The reference in the *Testament of Levi*, if this is a Christian passage, may be to the heavenly voice which acclaimed Jesus at his baptism. What concerns us here is the Abraham-Isaac reference. There is only one place in the patriarchal narrative where Abraham speaks to Isaac, and that is their interchange about the "lamb for a burnt-offering" as the two of them went together to the place of sacrifice in the land of Moriah (Gen. 22: 7 f.). This may be the occasion intended in John 8: 56 when Abraham rejoiced to see the day of Christ: it is difficult to think of a more appropriate one.

This was the exchange which led up to Jesus' affirmation, as the incarnation of the eternal Word, that he antedated Abraham: "Before Abraham was born, I am" (John 8: 58).


## 3. In the letter to the Galatians

John the Baptist and Jesus may imply that men and women who are not physically descended from Abraham may nevertheless be counted among his children, but the first person to claim this status expressly for Gentiles, so far as we know, is Paul.

Writing to the Galatians, he supports his insistence that men and women are justified before God by faith and not by the law by appealing to the example of Abraham. Abraham certainly had a highly meritorious record; Abraham, said God to Isaac, "obeyed my voice and kept my charge, my commandments, my statutes and my laws" (Gen. 26: 5). But when it comes to the ground of Abraham's justification, the biblical record is simple and unambiguous: Abraham "believed God, and it was reckoned to him as righteousness" (Gal. 3: 6). In view of the lines along which Paul proceeds to develop the argument, it is not immaterial to recall the circumstances in which this is recorded of Abraham. Abraham lamented his childless state, and Yahweh bade him turn his face up to the night sky, and see if he could count the stars. "So numerous will your offspring be", said Yahweh; and Abraham believed him, took him at his word (Gen. 15: 1–6).

We might pause a moment to consider whether this kind of faith is precisely that of which the gospel speaks. The faith which brings justification for the sinner, and leads to personal union with Christ, is total self-commitment to Christ, with an acceptance of all that God has done for us in him. But this includes believing what God has said. Conversely, Abraham's faith was reckoned to him for righteousness when he took God at his word and believed his promise, but this faith was part of Abraham's total self-commitment to the God who called him out of Ur and guided him throughout his subsequent life.

To revert to the abundant offspring promised to Abraham, who are they? Those who believe God, as Abraham did, says Paul. It is they who are justified, as believing Abraham was; it is they who receive the divine blessing, sharing it with believing Abraham.

The divine blessing which they share with Abraham is that of which God spoke when he said of him: "all the nations of the earth will bless themselves by him" (Gen. 18: 18). The RSV rendering "bless themselves" translates the reflexive conjugation of the Hebrew: it implies that when the nations desire a blessing for themselves they will say "May we be as blessed as Abraham was". But the reflexive conjugation can bear a passive sense, and this is the sense understood by the Septuagint version which Paul here quotes. Indeed, blessing to others through Abraham's blessing is pronounced in part of the divine promise to him in Gen. 12: 3, "I will bless those who bless you, and him who curses you I will curse" – words echoed by Balaam in Num. 24: 9, "Blessed be every one who blesses you, and cursed be every one who curses you."[4]

That the nations, which is as much as to say the Gentiles, would be blessed in Abraham was good news indeed for them, and this good news was announced in advance to Abraham when first he received the divine promise. "The scripture", says Paul, "foreseeing that God would justify the Gentiles by faith, preached the gospel beforehand to Abraham, saying, 'In you shall all the nations be blessed' " (Gal. 3: 8).

But Paul carries the argument farther: it is through Christ that this blessing is received by the Gentiles. The promise of blessing takes a variety of forms in the patriarchal narrative: the blessing is invoked or bestowed not only "in Abraham" but in his offspring. *"In your offspring"*, said God to Abraham after his faith was tried and proved in the matter of Isaac's sacrifice, "all the nations of the earth will bless themselves (or 'be blessed')" (Gen. 22: 18). The word "offspring" or "seed" is a collective singular:[5] it might denote one descendant or many. Which does it denote here? Both, says Paul: one and many – one, and therefore many; the many because of the one. That is the point of his curious argument: "It does not say, 'And to offsprings', referring to many; but, referring to one, 'And to your offspring,' which is Christ" (Gal. 3: 16). Paul has no wish to deny a plural significance to the collective noun; indeed, he makes the plural significance explicit as he goes on: "if you are Christ's, then you (plural) are Abraham's offspring" (Gal. 3: 29). But the fulfilment of the promise comes through Christ, who is Abraham's offspring in a distinctive sense, because it is through him that the blessing of Abraham is mediated to all believers, Gentile as

4. Cf. H. H. Rowley, *The Biblical Doctrine of Election* (London, 1950), pp. 65 ff.
5. Heb. *zera'*, Gk. σπέρμα.

well as Jewish, that they "might receive the promise of the Spirit through faith" (Gal. 3: 14). The argument, however, tracing the bestowal of the blessing through Christ, is admissible because of the use of a collective singular which could point to one descendant as readily as to many. If Christ is Abraham's offspring *par excellence*, then those who have been "baptized into Christ" are Abraham's offspring by union with Christ, and "heirs according to promise" of the blessing covenanted to Abraham.[6]

This marks a substantial advance on the use made of the same promise in the primitive apostolic preaching of Acts 3: 25 f.: "You are the sons of the prophets and of the covenant which God gave to your fathers, when he said to Abraham, 'In your offspring all the families of the earth will be blessed'. God, having raised up his Servant, sent him to you first, to bless you by turning every one of you from your wickedness". In these words of Peter to the people of Jerusalem, blessing for other families (even non-Israelite families) is not ruled out, but the blessing comes first to Peter's hearers and their kith and kin, because they are Abraham's offspring.

But are not Abraham's natural descendants his offspring? They are, Paul concedes, but not in the sense that matters most. In Gal. 4: 21–31 he illustrates the difference between Abraham's offspring "according to the flesh" and his offspring according to the promise by means of the story of Ishmael and Isaac: Ishmael, the product of human planning, and Isaac the child of promise, of whom it was said to Abraham, "In Isaac your offspring will be named" (Gen. 21: 13).[7] It must have been thought preposterous, and indeed scandalous, that Paul should correlate true-born Jews with

---

6. Gal. 3: 27, 29.

7. Cf. F. F. Bruce, " 'Abraham Had Two Sons': A Study in Pauline Hermeneutics", in *New Testament Studies: Essays in Honor of Ray Summers*, ed. H. L. Drumwright and C. Vaughan (Waco, 1975), pp. 71 ff.

the outcast father of the Ishmaelites while assigning to Gentile believers the blessing transmitted through Isaac, but such is the logic of Paul's argument. As he puts it later: "Not all are children of Abraham because they are his descendants, but 'Through Isaac shall your offspring be named'. This means that it is not the children of the flesh who are the children of God, but the children of the promise are reckoned as descendants" (Rom. 9: 7 f.).

### 4. In the letter to the Romans

Paul returns to Abraham's being justified by faith in his most systematic treatment of the subject in the early chapters of Romans. He has established the moral bankruptcy of both Gentiles and Jews before God, and spoken of the new way of righteousness held out to both alike for acceptance by faith – "being justified freely by his grace through the redemption which is in Christ Jesus" (Rom. 3: 24). Through the gospel God maintains his personal righteousness and acts as the justifier of circumcised and uncircumcised indiscriminately on the common ground of faith.

Then, in diatribe style, Paul asks what Abraham's situation is in this regard. True, if justification is achieved on the ground of works, Abraham could submit an impressive claim; but the testimony of scripture is that Abraham was justified by *faith*: he believed God, and it was reckoned to him for righteousness. Thus he whom Paul calls "our forefather according to the flesh" – i.e. (presumably) "the forefather of us Jews" – became in another sense the ancestor of all believers.

The argument is basically the same as that presented earlier to the Galatians, but Paul goes into greater detail in Romans, and in particular he makes two points which are absent from Galatians.

First, he points out that Abraham's faith was reckoned to him for righteousness while he was as yet uncircumcised. When he subsequently received circumcision, it was a seal of the righteousness-by-faith which he had received when he was still uncircumcised. Uncircumcised or circumcised, Abraham was equally a believer in God, and equally a recipient of the justification which comes by faith. Thus he is the father of *all* believers, uncircumcised and circumcised alike. The important matter is belief in God, not circumcision or uncircumcision.

Why did Paul not use this argument when writing to the Galatians? In some ways it could have been quite an effective answer to the circumcision party. We can hardly suppose that the argument did not occur to Paul's mind until some time between the writing of Galatians and Romans. It does not call for intensive Bible study to discover that the statement of Abraham's justification by faith comes rather earlier in Genesis than the inauguration of the rite of circumcision. But it might not have been expedient to use it in replying to the Galatians. They might have said, "Abraham was justified by faith; right, so were we. But Abraham was subsequently circumcised; right, that is what we are proposing for ourselves. You say that for Abraham circumcision was a seal of that righteousness-by-faith which he received while he was uncircumcised; right, why should it not have the same significance for us?"

Secondly, in discussing Abraham's justification by faith, Paul does not use Ishmael and Isaac to illustrate the two senses in which people might be called Abraham's offspring. Instead, he refers to the narrative of Genesis 17, where the patriarch's change of name from Abram to Abraham is associated with the divine promise: "I have made you father of a multitude (*'ab hamôn*) of nations". In what sense did Abraham become a father of many nations (Gentiles)? In the

spiritual sense, says Paul; that is to say, he is the father of all
the Gentiles who *believe*. While his being the father of his
natural descendants is associated with the promise of the
land of Canaan, wider dimensions are envisaged in relation
to his spiritual progeny: through the righteousness of faith
the promise came "to Abraham and his descendants, that
they should inherit the world" (Rom. 4: 13).

Then Paul enlarges on the quality of Abraham's faith in
God which was reckoned to him for righteousness. It was a
quite extraordinary faith, which set at defiance all known
canons of probability. God promised Abraham an abundant
posterity. Abraham weighed up all the factors in the situation: the long childlessness of Sarah and himself, his genera-
tive powers now "as good as dead" at such an advanced age,
Sarah's sterility and the fact that she had passed the age
when motherhood could be expected even in the most fertile
of women. He did not close his eyes to the facts: he faced
them all.[8] Yet on the other side he considered that God had
made him a promise, and that the one who promised was
equally able to perform. So he believed God, and the fact that
his belief was reckoned to him as righteousness has been
recorded, says Paul, for the encouragement of all who believe
in later ages: to us, he concludes (making the argument
personal), it will similarly be reckoned as righteousness "if
we believe in him who raised from the dead Jesus our Lord,
who was delivered up for our trespasses and raised for our
justification" (Rom. 4: 25).

### 5. *In the letter to the Hebrews*

In the letter to the Hebrews Abraham figures as a character in the Melchizedek drama and also (and more impor-

8. The force of this presentation is blunted by the insertion of "not" in the
Western and later texts of Rom. 4: 19, followed by AV: "he considered not his own
body now dead . . .".

tantly) as the one who above all others "received the promises" (Heb. 6: 13 ff.).[9] If in relation to Melchizedek he
plays a secondary rôle, this is in order to enhance the greatness of Melchizedek, not to diminish the importance of
Abraham. If even such a great man as Abraham accepted
Melchizedek's blessing and paid him tithes, Melchizedek
must be quite exceptionally great.

But we are concerned with Abraham's figuring in the
argument of Hebrews in his own right. In the list in chapter
11 of the men and women of old who won their record
through faith, more space is given to Abraham than to any
one else. "By faith Abraham obeyed when he was called to go
out to a place which he was to receive as an inheritance; and
he went out, not knowing where he was to go" (Heb. 11: 8).
But what was this place which he was to inherit? On one
plane the writer to the Hebrews accepts that the earthly
Canaan was the promised land where, like an alien,
Abraham "lived in tents with Isaac and Jacob, heirs with
him of the same promise" (Heb. 11: 9). But no earthly
Canaan can satisfy the man or woman who receives the
promises of God. If for Paul the land of Canaan is expanded
to "the world" as the inheritance of him who was to be
"father of a multitude of nations", for the writer to the
Hebrews it becomes "a better country, that is, a heavenly
one" (Heb. 11: 16).

This heavenly country, alternatively described by our
author as "the city which has the foundations, whose builder
and maker is God" (Heb. 11: 10), is that spiritual commonwealth in which all believing souls are enrolled as freeborn
citizens. Our author's insight was not at fault in discerning in

9. Cf. Heb. 7: 6. To "receive the promises" in this sense has a different meaning
from the language of Heb. 11: 13, 39 where it is said that the patriarchs and others
did not "receive the promises"; there the sense is that they did not (in mortal life)
receive the *fulfilment* of the promises (RSV "did not receive what was promised").

the promise to Abraham something more enduring than the fairest earthly possessions. To those who place their trust in God he gives possessions of real and incorruptible value. Since Abraham, Isaac and Jacob "live unto" God (Luke 20: 38), their true heritage is based in his eternal being; if they are the progenitors of the family of faith, their essential blessing cannot be different from those enjoyed by their spiritual children under the new covenant. "The Old Testament is not contrary to the New; for both in the Old and New Testament everlasting life is offered to mankind by Christ, who is the only mediator between God and man, being both God and man. Wherefore they are not to be heard, which feign that the old Fathers did look only for transitory promises . . .".[10] In death as in life Abraham was characterized by faith. His "pilgrim's progress" through this world had as its goal a home not of this world. Those who put their trust in God receive a *full* reward, and that reward, "the saints' everlasting rest", belongs inevitably to the eternal order which participates in the life of God. The faith of Abraham can thus serve as an example and incentive for men and women of faith in later ages: the heritage of glory to which they look forward through Christ is the heritage to which Abraham looked forward in his day.

One special instance of Abraham's faith singled out by the writer to the Hebrews is his offering up of Isaac. The "binding of Isaac" has been discerned by some students behind various New Testament passages;[11] but where it is not explicitly mentioned, any proposed reference to it must be problematical, as in John 8: 56 which we have considered.[12] But no doubt exists about the statement in Heb. 11: 17 that

10. Article VII of the Thirty-Nine Articles of Religion

11. Cf. H. J. Schoeps, *Paul: The Theology of the Apostle in the Light of Jewish Religious History* (London, 1961), pp. 141 ff.

12. See pp. 63 f.

"by faith Abraham, when he was tested, offered up Isaac, and he who had received the promises was ready to offer up his only son, of whom it was said, 'Through Isaac shall your descendants be named'."

The promises of God, which Abraham had accepted in faith, were bound up with the survival of Isaac. But the reconciliation of the promises with the command to offer up Isaac was God's problem, not Abraham's; Abraham's course was, now as ever, to comply obediently with the divine command. That Abraham expected to return from the place of sacrifice with Isaac is a reasonable inference from his words to the servants: "I and the lad will go yonder and worship, and we will come back to you" (Gen. 22: 5). If Isaac's life had to be taken, then Isaac's life had to be restored, if God's trustworthiness was to be vindicated. Of God's power to do this there was no question; neither was there in Abraham's mind any question of God's good faith. So far as Abraham was concerned, Isaac was as good as dead, and it was practically from the dead that he received him back – "in a figure", says our author, meaning perhaps in a manner prefiguring the resurrection of Christ.

## 6. *In the letter of James*

James also refers explicitly to the same incident when he wishes to show that Abraham's faith was manifested by his works. James chooses this rather than any other instance of Abraham's faith in God because it lends itself so well to the support of his argument that faith without works is dead. "You see how his faith was active along with his works, and faith was completed by works, and the scripture was fulfilled which says, 'Abraham believed God, and it was reckoned to him as righteousness', and he was called 'the friend of God' " (Jas. 2: 22 f.). The argument seems to be that, while

Abraham's acceptance of the divine promise regarding the birth of a son and heir was "reckoned to him as righteousness" according to the record of Gen. 15: 6, the reality of his faith was proved by his obedience when he was commanded to offer up Isaac, according to the later narrative of Gen. 22: 1–14. James's argument finds its basis in the words which conclude this narrative, where Yahweh (being able to swear by none greater) swears by himself[13] that the blessings promised to Abraham at his first call are re-confirmed and amplified to him and his descendants – "because you have done this, and have not withheld your son, your only son" (Gen. 22: 15 ff.). Abraham's faith was real faith, because it was based upon the unsupported word of God; it was real faith, because it was translated immediately into active obedience. It is those who show such faith as this that are "blessed with faithful Abraham" (Gal. 3: 9).

\* \* \* \* \* \*

The wide diversity of the New Testament writings which claim Abraham as the father of all believers suggests that this view of Abraham belongs to the most primitive stage of Christian teaching. Our Synoptic tradition, as we have seen, traces it back beyond Jesus himself to the preaching of John the Baptist, and it appears that John's words about God's ability to create new children of Abraham out of the most unlikely material were treated not as a mere ironical aside but as the adumbration of a truth which came to be realized in the early extension of the gospel among the Gentiles. In the acceptance of the gospel by them as well as by Israelite believers Abraham has become, in Paul's words, "the father of us all" (Rom. 4: 16).

13. Cf. Heb. 6: 13 ff.

CHAPTER IV


# A SHADOW OF GOOD THINGS TO COME

*(Hebrews 10: 1)*

CHAPTER IV

# A SHADOW OF GOOD THINGS TO COME

## *(Hebrews 10: 1)*

The law, says the writer to the Hebrews (thinking more particularly of the Old Testament law of sacrifices and related ceremonies) had "a shadow of good things to come, not the very image of the things" (Heb. 10: 1). In these words he summed up a substantial part of his more detailed exposition of the relation between law and gospel.

## 1. Shadow and substance

The author of the letter to the Hebrews is not the only New Testament writer to make use of the shadow/substance analogy. Paul expresses himself to much the same effect in writing to the Colossians, when he says that the whole system of regulations concerning food, drink, festivals and sacred days is "a shadow of things to come, but the substance (he adds) is Christ's" (Col. 2: 17). The word he uses for "substance" is *sōma* ("body"), which appears elsewhere in Hellenistic Jewish literature (e.g. in Philo[1] and Josephus[2]) as

---

1. "It is preposterous that shadow (σκιά) should be preferred to substance (σώματα) or a copy (μίμημα) to originals (ἀρχέτυπα)" (Philo, *Migration of Abraham*, 12).

2. Archelaus came to Rome "to ask Augustus for the shadow (σκιά) of kingship, when he had already seized the substance (σῶμα)" (Josephus, *Jewish War* ii. 28).

the antithesis to *skia* ("shadow"). But in view of Paul's
earlier identification in the same letter of the "body of
Christ" with the church (Col. 1: 18, 24), it is inevitable that
we should relate the clause "the substance (body) is
Christ's" to his concept of the church. Perhaps he means that
the reality which was foreshadowed by the now obsolete
ceremonial economy is the new order whose distinctive fea-
ture is that believers of the most diverse origins – Jews,
Gentiles or whatnot – are alike united by faith to Christ,
incorporated into him by the Spirit. To adhere now to the
ceremonial regulations of a bygone age is to fail to grasp this
new order, to fail (in other words) to "hold fast to the Head,
by whom the whole body is equipped and supplied through
its joints and ligaments and thus increases with the increase
of God" (Col. 2: 18 f.).

T. W. Manson based an interesting argument regarding
the date and purpose of the letter to the Hebrews on certain
resemblances which he discerned between it and the letter to
the Colossians.[3] Without endorsing his conclusion – that the
letter to the Hebrews was sent to a community in the Lycus
valley to deal with a situation in which the so-called "Colos-
sian heresy" had not developed to the stage reflected in
Paul's letter to the same area – I content myself with drawing
attention to this remarkable point of contact between the two
documents.

To revert to Heb. 10: 1, here the antithesis to "shadow"
(*skia*) is not "body" (*sōma*) but "image" (*eikōn*) or, as the
RSV rendering runs, "the true *form* of the realities". The
"image" or "form", it is implied, partakes of the essence of
the reality in a way that the shadow does not. In appropriate
contexts, indeed, the *eikōn* could denote a *mere* copy of the
original, and this is how *eikōn* in our present passage appears

3. T. W. Manson, *Studies in the Gospels and Epistles* (Manchester, 1962), pp. 252 ff.

to have been taken by the editor or scribe responsible for the aberrant reading in our earliest extant manuscript – papyrus 46 – where the law is said to have "a shadow of the good things to come and the image of the things".[4] In this reading *eikōn* is practically synonymous with *skia*, but in spite of its antiquity the reading cannot be accepted: the construction of the sentence demands that *eikōn* and *skia* be contrasted, not practically identified.[5] The reading of papyrus 46 leads the reader to expect some positive affirmation of the value of the law; the negative assessment which is actually made in the principal clause – the law's inability to make the worshippers "perfect" – demands something like the reading of our other witnesses.

An analogy to the contrast between *skia* and *eikōn* is found by G. Kittel in an incident recorded in the Babylonian Talmud. Rabbi Banna'ah, it is said, inspected the tombs of the patriarchs, and when he entered the tomb of Adam a *bat qôl* said to him: "You have looked on the likeness of my image; you may not look on my image itself!"[6] (The Aramaic word translated "image" is a loanword from the Greek *eikōn*.) The *bat qôl* is the echo of the voice of God, in whose image Adam was made: to look on Adam's dead body was not the same thing as looking on the image of God. Professor G. Zuntz adduces a passage from Iamblichus, in which that writer urges "a turning from the shadows to the images and the light".[7] Here the images are essential forms of the reality,

---

4. For οὐκ αὐτὴν τὴν εἰκόνα papyrus 46 has καὶ τὴν εἰκόνα.

5. Cf. G. Zuntz, *The Text of the Epistles* (London, 1953), pp. 20 ff. Thus, εἰκών is much more substantial than ὑπόδειγμα ("copy"), which is combined with σκιά in Heb. 8: 5, where the material tabernacle is "a copy and shadow of the heavenly sanctuary" (cf. the similar use of ὑπόδειγμα, "copy", in Heb. 9: 23).

6. *TDNT* iii, p. 395 (*s.v.* εἰκών), with reference to TB *Baba Batra* 58a. Banna'ah flourished towards the end of the second century A.D.

7. *The Text of the Epistles*, p. 22, quoting Iamblichus, *On the Common Mathematics*, 6 (Teubner edition [Leipzig, 1891], p. 28), where, however, εἴδωλον, not εἰκών, is the word for "image". For εἰκών we might compare Philo, *Life of Moses* ii. 51,

and not mere shadows of it.

The outstanding instance of the shadow analogy in Greek literature is the parable of the cave at the beginning of the seventh book of Plato's *Republic*.[8] Plato envisages a company of people compelled to live in a cave with their backs to the entrance, so that the only conception they can form of the outside world is derived from shadows on the wall which they are obliged to face. By such unfortunate people, the world of shadows would be taken for the real world, and indeed any talk of a real world outside in the sunshine would be dismissed by them as a fantastic myth. A modern Plato might use the picture of people compelled to live in a cinema, or to stay glued before the television screen, and indeed such a picture would not be shrugged off as too absurd today. Do we not know of people who have difficulty in distinguishing television programmes from real life – who indeed think that what they see on the screen *is* real life? "It's true", they say, "I saw it on the 'telly'."

In Plato's parable the cave-dwellers correspond to people living in the material and phenomenal world: the shadows are the objects which they perceive with their senses, which indeed they take to be the ultimate realities. But for Plato the ultimate realities are the "ideas" or archetypes eternally existing in the supercelestial realm,[9] conceived by the mind; of them the objects perceived by the senses are but material, imperfect and passing copies. It is, however, just as difficult to persuade *l'homme moyen sensuel* of the existence of that eternal order as it would be to persuade the fancied cave-

where Moses is said to have regarded his law-code as "an image (εἰκών) most truly corresponding to the constitution of the world", or Josephus, *Jewish War* v. 212, where the screen at the entrance to Jerusalem temple is called "an image (εἰκών) of the universe" – but in both these places there is a contrast between the image and that of which it is an image.

8. Plato, *Republic* vii. 514a–517a.

9. Plato, *Phaedrus* 247c.

dweller of the reality of the world outside his cave.

## 2 Sanctuary and sacrifice

To the writer to the Hebrews the antithesis between substance and shadow is not only – and perhaps not mainly – the antithesis between the upper and the lower, the heavenly and earthly realms; it is pre-eminently the antithesis between the new and the old.

The antithesis between the upper and lower realms is certainly present to his mind; indeed, he finds it anticipated in the Old Testament text where Moses is commanded to make all the details of the wilderness tabernacle "after the pattern for them, which is being shown you on the mountain" (Exod. 25: 40). The implication of these words is that Moses was shown something like a scale-model of the sanctuary which was to be built; the Greek noun *typos*, quoted by our author from the Septuagint, represents Hebrew *tabnît*, meaning "building" or "construction". But our author understands something more than this: to him the material shrine erected by Moses (or under his direction) was an earthly reproduction of the heavenly, immaterial dwelling-place of God. The author of Wisdom, writing a century or so earlier than the writer to the Hebrews, expresses a similar view of Solomon's temple, when he makes Solomon in prayer to God speak of his temple as "a copy[10] of the holy tent which thou didst prepare from the beginning" (Wisdom 9: 8).

The idea of the earthly sanctuary, in which the deity dwells after a token fashion, as the copy of his true, heavenly dwelling, has an ancestry which goes back far earlier than Plato. It has ancient Near Eastern antecedents: in the Babylonian *Enuma Elish*, for example, there is a heavenly

10. Gk. μίμημα ("imitation"); cf. Philo's use of this word as quoted on p. 77, n. 1, and Josephus's use of μίμησις as quoted on p. 82, n. 12.

"court of assembly" which is the archetype of the earthly temple.[11] That this idea survived into the Christian era is evident from the cosmic interpretations which Josephus places on details of the wilderness tabernacle and the Jerusalem temple – far-fetched though many of his interpretations may appear to be.[12]

But the writer to the Hebrews is concerned to emphasize the contrast between past and present at least as much as that between the higher and the lower. The law had a shadow of the good things that were to come; the decisive transition from shadow to reality is marked by the advent of Christ as "high priest of the good things that have come" (Heb. 9: 11).[13]

The relation of the sacrificial ritual of the old order to the work of Christ is set forth in the form of an exposition of Psalm 40: 6–8. The psalmist expresses his devotion to the will of God, in the firm assurance that such heart-obedience is much more acceptable to God than all animal sacrifices and the like:

> Sacrifice and offering thou dost not desire;
>> but thou hast given me an open ear.
> Burnt offering and sin-offering
>> thou hast not required.
> Then I said, "Lo, I come;
>> in the roll of the book it is written of me;
> I delight to do thy will, O my God;
>> thy law is within my heart".

11. Akkadian *ubshukkinaku* (*Enuma Elish* 3: 61, 119, 131); cf. A. Heidel, *The Babylonian Genesis* (Chicago, ²1951), pp. 33, 35; W. F. Albright, *Archaeology and the Religion of Israel* (Baltimore, ³1953), pp. 142 ff.; also R. E. Clements, *God and Temple* (Oxford, 1965).

12. Cf. Josephus, *Antiquities* iii. 123, 180 ff. In both passages he sees the threefold division of the tabernacle area – outer court, holy place and holy of holies – as a copy (μίμησις) of the cosmic system, with sea and land accessible to all but heaven reserved for God.

13. The variant reading "good things to come" at Heb. 9: 11 (cf. AV) is due to the influence of Heb. 10: 1.

The four words for sacrifice are perhaps used by way of stylistic variation, according to the regular pattern of Hebrew parallelism, like "sacrifice" (*zebaḥ*) and "burnt-offering (*'ôlāh*) in Ps. 51: 16. Yet perhaps it is not accidental that between them they cover the main types of levitical sacrifice. "Sacrifice" (*zebaḥ*) is used not only in a general sense but also, more particularly, as a synonym for the "peace-offering" or "shared offering" (*shelāmîm*); "offering" (*minḥāh*) is used not only as a general term for "present" but also, in the levitical code, as the special name of the "meal offering" or "cereal offering". "Burnt offering" (*'ôlāh*) and sin-offering" (*ḥeṭā'āh*) speak for themselves. So the psalmist sweeps all the acknowledged categories of ritual sacrifice aside and asserts that what God desires is obedient hearts and lives. The will of God is recorded in two forms: externally, "in the roll of the book", and inwardly in his servant's heart, so that his life is the translation into practice of the written law. The terms of Jeremiah's new covenant have come true in his experience; he has fulfilled the deuteronomic injunction: "these words which I command you this day shall be upon your heart" (Deut. 6: 6), possibly in a deeper sense than their original intention, which may simply have been, "you shall memorize them" (learn them by heart, as we say).

Our psalmist was by no means alone in this among Old Testament writers: we may think of the authors of Psalms 50 and 51, not to speak of the prophets Amos, Micah, Isaiah and Jeremiah.[14] So long as the sanctuary stood, the sacrificial order maintained its central place in the national worship; yet there were times when it became evident that true religion could get on very well without it. Such were the periods of the Babylonian exile and the three years in the

14. Cf. Psalm 50: 9 ff.; 51: 16 f.; Amos 5: 21 ff.; Mic. 6: 6 ff.; Isa. 1: 11 ff.; Jer. 7: 21 ff.

second century B.C. during which the temple was turned
over to a pagan cult, "the abomination of desolation".[15] And
in fact the circumstances of life in the Jewish dispersion
showed that religious life could function without the temple
and sacrifices. But it could not function at all without obedience to the will of God: that is the very heart of true religion.

The writer to the Hebrews expresses this conviction in his
exposition of the words of Psalm 40. He quotes them according to the Septuagint version, and he interprets them as
spoken by the Son of God in prospect of his incarnation and
life on earth (Heb. 10: 5 ff.):

Consequently, at his coming into the world, he says:

"Sacrifices and offerings thou hast not desired,
but a body hast thou prepared for me;
in burnt offerings and sin offerings thou hast taken no
pleasure.
Then I said, 'Lo, I have come to do thy will, O God',
as it is written of me in the roll of the book".

The Septuagint replaces the Hebrew "ears hast thou opened
for me" by "a body hast thou prepared for me". This is a
paraphrase, in which the part is replaced by the whole. The
hollowing out of ears is part of the work of fashioning a body.
The Septuagint paraphrase lent itself admirably to the purpose of our author, who interpreted it of the incarnation of
Christ. But if the Hebrew wording had been reproduced
literally by the Greek translator, it would have served his
purpose equally well, for the ears are the organs of hearing,
and hence of obeying. This is the reason for their special
mention in the original text of the psalm, as it is also in the

15. 1 Macc. 1: 54; this was the Jews' mocking pun on Ba'al Shamen ("the lord of
heaven"), the Syrian counterpart of Olympian Zeus (cf. Dan. 9: 27; 11: 31; 12: 11).

third Isaianic servant song, where the Servant says of God (Isa. 50: 4 f.):

> Morning by morning he wakens,
>   he wakens my ear
>   to hear as those who are taught.
> The Lord God has opened my ear,
>   and I was not rebellious,
>   I turned not backwards.

The obedience to which all true servants of God dedicate themselves was manifested in perfection by Jesus, whom our author envisages as the speaker in Psalm 40: 6–8. The various forms of ritual sacrifice are ineffective in themselves: what they could not achieve has been achieved by the only truly acceptable and effective sacrifice – the spontaneous sacrifice of a life totally obedient to the will of God. And by the will of God, accomplished in the life and supremely in the death of Jesus – the offering of his body – his people are "sanctified".

### 3. Access to God

What is true of sacrifice is true of other ceremonial institutions of the old order, such as the cleansing rites which were prescribed for acceptable access to God. Among these the writer singles out the preparation of purifying water (*mê niddāh*) with the ashes of the red heifer.[16] He concedes that such a cleansing medium may effectively remove defilement which is external and material like itself. Just what kind of defilement he thought it did in practice remove we may wonder, but he does not tell us: that is not what interests him.

16. Num. 19: 1 ff.

Ceremonial defilement was reckoned to be something which impaired one's relation with God or impeded access to him, but our author insists that the only kind of pollution which does this is inward and spiritual: it is the *conscience* that needs to be cleansed from "dead works" – works which lead to death – or from anything else that pollutes it if men and women are to be set free "to serve the living God". No external cleansing agent can do this: the one effective means of purifying the conscience is "the blood of Christ, who through the eternal Spirit offered himself a spotless sacrifice to God" (Heb. 9: 14). The blood of Christ is not understood here materially: how could it be? It denotes the offering up in death of a life wholly dedicated to the will of God, a life characterized by unspotted holiness. This sacrifice was offered up in the spiritual realm; it is, as the New English Bible puts it, "a spiritual and eternal sacrifice". How much more is implied in the phrase "through the eternal Spirit" is uncertain: since, when Yahweh first introduces his Servant in Isa. 42: 1, he says, "I have put my Spirit upon him", it may be implied that all the Servant's ministry, and pre-eminently the self-oblation as a sin-offering which crowns his ministry, is accomplished through the divine Spirit. In that self-oblation the Servant fills the twofold rôle of priest and victim, as Christ does in the letter to the Hebrews. Thus (to quote James Denney) "in Christ's sacrifice we see the final revelation of what God is, that behind which there is nothing in God, so that the religion which rests on that sacrifice rests on the ultimate truth of the divine nature, and can never be shaken".[17]

What is true of the cleansing efficacy of the blood of Christ is equally true of its sacrificial efficacy, especially when the sacrifice in view is the sin-offering. As it is impossible for the

17. J. Denney, *The Death of Christ* (London, [1902] 1951), p. 119.

material "water of purification" to remove an inward stain, so it is impossible that animal sacrifice, "the blood of bulls and goats", should take away sin. The blood of Christ betokens a sacrifice offered in the spiritual realm, by which not only is his people's conscience cleansed from pollution but their sins are expiated and access is opened up for them into the presence of God.

The faithful worshipper of God always knew himself to be welcome in the divine presence. The psalmist who said, "For me it is good to be near God" (Psalm 73: 28) was not concerned about ritual fitness for approaching him. But our author is thinking of the priestly and sacrificial structure of the earthly sanctuary, where everything spoke of the *difficulty* of approaching the throne-room of God. The nearer to that throne-room one approached, the more prohibitive were the barriers and the fewer the people who were permitted to pass through them. The elaborately detailed prescription of the tabernacle services and furnishings in Exodus constituted an object-lesson, showing that "the way into the sanctuary was not yet open while the first tabernacle retained its status" (Heb. 9: 8).

## 4. Continuing relevance of the shadow?

The shadow, then, is very defective as compared with the "very image" or substance of man's relation to God. If the Aaronic priesthood, the earthly sanctuary and the levitical sacrifices are as ineffective as our author argues, then the relation of the shadow to the substance is much more one of contrast than resemblance. If this is so, how should the closing chapters of Exodus and the opening chapters of Leviticus be read by Christians? There is one interpretative tradition which by allegorization seeks – and finds – analogies in the minutest details of the sacrificial regulations

and tabernacle arrangements to the work of Christ on earth
and now in heaven. I need mention only Andrew Bonar's
*Commentary on Leviticus* or C. H. Mackintosh's *Notes on the
Pentateuch* to illustrate what I have in mind. One difficulty I
have with this approach is that, in the absence of exegetical
controls, it encourages unfettered fantasy. If a preacher
chooses to employ some aspect of these prescriptions to
illustrate a point he wishes to make in expounding the gospel, good and well. But if he says, or implies, that this was
God's intention in giving these instructions to Moses and
Aaron, I must part company with him. Or when it is suggested that the risen Lord, expounding the scriptures to the
two disciples on the Emmaus road, may have shown them
how he personally fulfilled the details of the levitical offerings, I can only say that this is not what I understand by
biblical exegesis or historical probability.

When Andrew Bonar, for example, finds a spiritual
analogue to the "memorial portion" of the meal offering of
Lev. 2: 2 in Cornelius's prayers and alms, which ascended as
a "memorial" into the presence of God (Acts 10: 4), we can
follow him. Cornelius's "dedication of self and substance,
expressed by prayers and alms", he says, "was acknowledged on the part of God by the gift of more light and
liberty."[18] When he speaks of this "memorial portion" of the
meal offering, garnished with frankincense and oil, as a
picture of the perfect self-dedication of our Lord, the same
principle of interpretation must be acknowledged; "when
Christ", he says, "presented his humanity and all associated
therewith, he was indeed *fragrant* to the Father, and the oil of
the Spirit was on him above his fellows".[19] But the allegorization of the frankincense and the oil, implicit in these
words, must be held in check. If not, we find the details of the

18. A. A. Bonar, *A Commentary on the Book of Leviticus* (London, [4]1861), p. 38.
19. Bonar, p. 37.

preparation of this offering treated as setting forth the passion of our Lord: the *"ears of corn"* in the voluntary meal offering of Lev. 2: 14 are "a figure of Christ":

> They are *"dried by the fire"*, to represent Jesus feeling the wrath of his Father ... It was thus that the only pure humanity that ever walked on the plains of earth was wasted away during three-and-thirty years by the heat of wrath he had never deserved. While obeying night and day, with all his soul and strength, the burning wrath of God was drying up his frame. *"Beaten out of full ears"*, represents the bruises and strokes by which he was prepared for the altar.[20]

On this it must be said that not only is the allegorization doubtful, but the alleged reality to which the allegory points is more doubtful still – it is, in fact, completely unacceptable. The moral lesson which is drawn from all this is acceptable in itself:

> We must be conformed to Jesus in all things: and here it is taught us that we must be conformed to him in self-dedication – self-renunciation. We must please the Father; as he left us an example, saying, "I do always those things that please him" (John viii. 29), even under the blackest sky.[21]

But that the prescriptions for the meal offering were designed to convey this lesson I cannot easily believe.

I have, with great respect, quoted Andrew Bonar because he belonged to the main stream of Reformed orthodoxy, and could not be dismissed as though he represented a tradition of typological eccentricity.

Certain popular Bible teachers specialize in this typological ministry, and make it more graphic by the use of a

20. Bonar, p. 46.
21. Bonar, pp. 46 f.

scale-model of the wilderness tabernacle. There are some who observe proper exegetical discipline when they do this; but when listening to many I have never understood how they could be so sure of their interpretations. For example, five horizontal bars of acacia wood ran round three sides of the tabernacle to support the uprights. The middle bar ran continuously all the way round, and it has been inferred (unnecessarily) from Exod. 26: 28 and 36: 33 that, unlike the other four, it was hidden from sight. The architectural function of these bars is clearly to be understood. Have they any other function – a theological or a "typical" one? I doubt it. One suggestion I have come across is that the four visible bars represent the quadrilateral of Acts 2: 42 – the apostles' teaching and fellowship, the breaking of bread and the prayers – while the middle one represents "the unity of the Spirit in the bond of peace" (Eph. 4: 3). But what status has any such interpretation, except that at most it is a "nice thought", suitable (it may be conceded) for homiletic or devotional purposes?

Again, external light (it has been inferred from the record) was excluded as far as possible from the tabernacle, which was illuminated by the seven oil-lamps of the *menorah*. I have known this to be made to teach that for the worship of God divine light alone is adequate; man-made illumination must be rejected. But it is unlikely that the light of the sun should, for any Old Testament believer, represent man-made illumination, while oil-lamps should be regarded as divine light. I know that some will appeal to the use of oil as a symbol of the Holy Spirit; it is worth pointing out that it is oil when used for *anointing* that symbolizes the Spirit.

The instances I have cited may be thought to be extreme: I could have cited others more extreme still. What I want to suggest is that the allegorizing of this element in the Pentateuch is uncalled for and does nothing to explain the text.

Such allegorizing was current in the first century A.D.; we have only to think of Philo's treatment of all these details.[22] Even Josephus inherited an allegorical tradition on which he draws in his description of the temple.[23] How far the writer to the Hebrews went in this direction we cannot say: when he remarks that he "cannot now speak in detail" of the articles of furniture in the tabernacle (Heb. 9: 5) we could wish that he had left us his thoughts on the subject elsewhere. What he does tell us is that the order represented by the tabernacle is self-evidently inadequate by contrast with the new order introduced by Christ. Christ, for example, has accomplished for all time by his one sacrifice of himself what the annual sin-offering of the Day of Atonement, presented in the earthly holy of holies, never even began to accomplish. It is not the analogy, but the difference, between the ritual of the Day of Atonement and the work of Christ that the writer to the Hebrews emphasizes.

The shadow bears witness to the substance, indeed, but one could form at best a very imperfect idea of the substance if one had only the shadow as a guide. There was a historic moment in the history of Anglican evangelicalism when, in Passion Week of 1779, Charles Simeon read in Bishop Wilson's work on the Lord's Supper the statement that "the Jews knew what they did, when they transferred their sin to the head of their offering". But what was it that they "knew", in the days when the sin-offering was regularly offered? We may suspect that Bishop Wilson read into their "knowledge" something of his own knowledge of the "substance" of which the levitical sin-offering was a "shadow". Charles Simeon himself certainly did so: he knew what the "substance" was, although he had not hitherto fully appreciated his own interest in that "substance". As he read Wilson's words, "the

22. Cf. Philo, *Life of Moses* ii. 71 ff.
23. Josephus, *Jewish War* v. 212 ff.

thought came into my mind", he tells us, "What, may I transfer all my guilt to another? Has God provided an Offering for me, that I may lay my sins on His head? Then, God willing, I will not bear them on my own soul one moment longer. Accordingly I sought to lay my sins upon the sacred head of Jesus".[24]

It was Charles Simeon's knowledge of the New Testament gospel that led him so unerringly to Jesus as the bearer and remover of his people's sins. The "shadow" provided the idiom in which he expressed his thought, but his thought could not have been conceived apart from the gospel revelation.

It is interesting, however, to observe that the particular aspect of the "shadow" which provided him with his idiom is one which does not figure in the Epistle to the Hebrews. Wilson and Simeon may have had in mind the sin-offering brought by "one of the common people" (Lev. 4: 27 ff.); but in that ritual the person who brought the sacrificial animal not only laid his hand on it but also killed it. It is not expressly said that he laid his sins on it, as the high priest put the people's *sins* on the scapegoat in the ritual of the Day of Atonement. When the writer to the Hebrews deals with the ritual of the Day of Atonement he concentrates on that part of the ritual which deals with the high priest's ministry in the holy of holies. The animal whose blood was presented there was the goat of expiation, not the scapegoat ("the goat for Azazel") which carried the people's sins away into the wilderness. But it was on to the scapegoat's head that the sins of the people were transferred.[25]

---

24. Cf. H. C. G. Moule, *Charles Simeon* (London, [1892] 1948), pp. 25 f. The work which Simeon read was the *Short and Plain Instructions for the Better Understanding of the Lord's Supper*, by Thomas Wilson, bishop of Sodor and Man (London, 1736).

25. For the relation of the scapegoat to New Testament teaching cf. L. L. Morris, "The Day of Atonement and the Work of Christ", *Reformed Theological Review* 14 (1955), pp. 9 ff.

In the ritual for the Day of Atonement, indeed, we may have the bringing together of two originally separate rites involving a goat – one sacrificial, the other apotropaic – either of which independently was reckoned to deal effectively with the sins of the community. The sacrifice of the one goat made atonement for the sanctuary, when its blood was sprinkled on and in front of the mercy-seat, as well as for the whole assembly of Israel (Lev. 16: 16 f.); the expulsion of the other goat, on to which the sins of the community had been unloaded, ensured purification by the removal into the wilderness of those defiling elements.

By the first century A.D. it was believed that the ritual was calculated "to avert and serve as an expiation for the sins of the whole people"[26] – not by any inherent efficacy, perhaps, but because this was the decree of the Holy One.[27] But this belief is ruled out by the writer to the Hebrews as impossible: "it is impossible", he says, "that the blood of bulls and goats should take away sins" (Heb. 10: 4). The blood of bulls and goats, in his eyes, is an ineffective shadow, like everything else associated with the earthly and temporary sanctuary. Whether he envisaged any more effective "very image" or "true form" of the reality, apart from the reality itself, he does not say, but clearly he did not. Only in the reality could the "true form" of the good things to come be seen. The Holy One does indeed decree the removal of his people's sins and their cleansing from inward defilement, but his decree is made effective by a sacrifice that is inherently efficacious – the self-sacrifice of the one who perfectly fulfilled his Father's will, in death as in life, and who thus "by a single

26. Josephus, *Antiquities* iii. 241.
27. Cf. Yoḥanan ben Zakkai's comment on the water of purification prepared from the ashes of the red heifer: "neither does a dead body defile, nor does water purify; but the Holy One, blessed be he, says: 'I have laid down a statute, I have issued a decree; you shall not transgress my decree' " (*Numbers Rabba* 19: 8 on Num. 19: 2).

offering" has not only himself "been made perfect for ever" as his people's high priest but "has perfected for all time those who are sanctified" (Heb. 7: 28; 10: 14). In other words, the sacrifice of Jesus has completely fitted him to be his people's representative in the presence of God, and by that same sacrifice his people are completely fitted to enter the presence of God through him.

# THE SPIRIT OF PROPHECY

*(Revelation 19: 10)*

# THE SPIRIT OF PROPHECY

*(Revelation 19: 10)*

The witness-bearing rôle of the Spirit of God is a recurring theme in the New Testament. "When the Paraclete comes ...", says Jesus to his disciples in the upper room, "he will bear witness to me; and you also are witnesses, because you have been with me from the beginning" (John 15: 26 f.). To much the same effect is the apostles' affirmation to the Sanhedrin in Acts 5: 32 as they assert the fact and significance of Jesus' resurrection: "we are witnesses to these things, and so is the Holy Spirit, whom God has given to those who obey him." (It is interesting, by the way, to compare the promises about the Spirit's ministry in the upper-room discourses of the Fourth Gospel and the record of his ministry in Acts, from the day of Pentecost onwards; there is a remarkable correspondence in this respect between the two documents.)[1]

## 1. Prophetic Witness in the New Testament

The witness of the Spirit with and in the witness of those whom he indwells and empowers does not, however, exhaust

---

1. Cf. W. F. Lofthouse, "The Holy Spirit in the Acts and the Fourth Gospel", *Expository Times* 52 (1940–41), pp. 334 ff.

his witness-bearing rôle. The early Christians were fully conscious that the writings of the Old Testament prophets, to which they appealed so regularly in support of their message, formed another aspect of the Spirit's ministry. Jeremiah's new covenant oracle is quoted by the writer to the Hebrews as the Holy Spirit's witness (Heb. 10: 15–17), just as the warning words of Psalm 95 and the prescriptions for the tabernacle and its services are ascribed to him (Heb. 3: 7; 9: 8). If Peter in the house of Cornelius could declare that Christ is the one to whom "all the prophets bear witness" (Acts 10: 43), it is made plain in 1 Peter 1: 10 f. that in their witness "the Spirit of Christ within them was bearing witness in advance to the sufferings of Christ and the glories that were to follow".[2]

If the Spirit of prophecy is here called "the Spirit of Christ", the reference could be more particularly to those Old Testament passages cast in the first person singular in which early Christians discerned their Lord as speaking before his incarnation;[3] but in general the Spirit of prophecy is conceived in the New Testament as the Spirit of *messianic* prophecy, foretelling through the prophets what was to be fulfilled with the passion and triumph of the Messiah.

But the early church experienced the Spirit of prophecy in a new way. The same Spirit as had in days gone by spoken through the Old Testament prophets was now speaking in the church through prophets of the new era. We have references in the narrative of Acts to Agabus and other prophets not only speaking by the Spirit (11: 28; 21: 4) but claiming his authority for their utterances: "Thus says the Holy Spirit

---

2. See p. 106.
3. Cf. the quotation of Psalm 40: 6–8 in Heb. 10: 5–7 (see p. 84); also 1 Clement 22: 1, where a quotation from Psalm 34 (LXX 33): 11–17 is introduced by the words: "All these things are confirmed by faith in Christ, for he himself through the Holy Spirit encourages us as follows".

..." (21: 11). The prophetic utterances recorded in Acts appear to have had a temporary and *ad hoc* reference. Something of more abiding value is probably implied in the gift of prophecy so highly recommended by Paul to the Corinthians; the exercise of this gift involves the declaration of the mind of God in the power of the Spirit so compellingly manifested that the church is built up and unbelievers convicted of the reality of the divine presence.[4] This is the gift which in the letter to the Ephesians (2: 20; cf. 3: 5; 4: 11) is set alongside the gift of apostleship as belonging to the church's foundation.

It is widely believed that such prophets spoke in the name of the exalted Lord and that, when they did so, his authority was attached to what they said. This may well be so; in that case we can appreciate the care with which both Paul and John in their respective epistles direct that prophetic utterances in church must be intelligently evaluated and accepted only if their testimony to Christ is unexceptionable – Paul insisting on the acknowledgment that Jesus is Lord (1 Cor. 12: 1–3) and John on the confession of his real incarnation (1 John 4: 1–3).

Sometimes, however, it is argued that the first-century churches were not greatly concerned to distinguish the words of the early Jesus, preserved by tradition, from those of the risen Lord, spoken through prophets – so much so that words of the latter category might be given a context in the historical ministry and recorded in the Gospels.[5]

It is true that occasionally in the Gospels we come upon a saying of Jesus which is more applicable to his relationship

---

4. Cf. 1 Cor. 14: 24 f.

5. Cf. N. Perrin, *Rediscovering the Teaching of Jesus* (London, 1967), p. 15 ("The early Church made no attempt to distinguish between the words the earthly Jesus had spoken and those spoken by the risen Lord through a prophet in the community"); but see D. Hill, "On the Evidence for the Creative Rôle of Christian Prophets", *NTS* 20 (1973–74), pp. 262 ff.

with his people after his exaltation than in the course of his historical ministry, such as "where two or three are gathered in my name, there am I in the midst of them" (Matt. 18: 20). The paragraph of which this forms the concluding sentence, with its ruling on the course to be followed within the *ekklēsia* when a brother commits some sin (verses 15 ff.), belongs to the category of "sentences of holy law in the New Testament" whose origin Ernst Käsemann finds in prophetic proclamation in the church and which, because of this origin and their eschatological orientation, he distinguishes from the later formulations of canon law.[6]

But in general the early Christians appear to have been backward in devising or discerning dominical rulings on some of the issues which were most keenly debated among them. It has often been pointed out that Paul, who readily cites as authoritative sayings of Jesus bearing on questions which arose in his churches, has no idea of creating such sayings where they had not been "delivered" to him, distinguishing, for instance, in matters of marriage and divorce an absolutely authoritative charge which "not I but the Lord" gives from less binding counsel which "I say, not the Lord" (1 Cor. 7: 10, 12). And whereas much space is given in the Gospels to words of Jesus about sabbath observance, which was much more of an issue in the context of his ministry than in the early church, no ruling of his is recorded which could have a bearing on the circumcision controversy, which was so live at one stage in the church's Gentile mission but could not have arisen during his Palestinian activity. Yet, if dominical "sentences of holy law" were created so freely as is sometimes suggested, by prophetic utterance or otherwise, this is the kind of issue on which we should expect to find them cited.

6. E. Käsemann, "Sentences of Holy Law in the New Testament", E.T. in *New Testament Questions of Today* (London, 1969), pp. 66 ff.

## 2. *The testimony of Jesus*

The one New Testament writing, however, which above all others is germane to this matter is that which, almost in its entirety, is the product of such prophecy: the Revelation to John. The Revelation certainly claims to communicate a message from the risen Christ. Its contents are called "the words of this prophecy" (Rev. 1: 3); those to whom they are addressed are expected to recognize in them "what the Spirit says to the churches" (Rev. 2: 7, etc.). The words themselves constitute "the testimony of Jesus"; indeed, "the testimony of Jesus is the Spirit of prophecy" (Rev. 19: 10). So said the interpreting angel to John when refusing his well-meant but misplaced homage.

In the phrase, "the testimony of Jesus", the genitive, "of Jesus", is most probably objective, as it is in the preceding clause of Rev. 19: 10 where the angel declines to accept John's homage on the ground, as he says, that "I am a fellow-servant with you and your brethren who hold the testimony of Jesus", and also as it certainly is in Rev. 17:6, where "the witnesses of Jesus"[7] are put to death by the scarlet woman. True, Jesus himself is "the faithful witness" (Rev. 1: 5; cf. 3: 14) and the whole Apocalypse is his testimony to his people (Rev. 22: 16, 20). But they in their turn are his witnesses, like Antipas the Pergamene martyr, whom he calls "my faithful witness" (Rev. 2: 13), or indeed like John himself, exiled to Patmos for "the word of God and the testimony of Jesus",[8] where he was entrusted with the revelation which the humiliated but now exalted Christ received from God "to show his servants what must soon take place"

---

7. Here and in the reference to Antipas in Rev. 2: 13 Gk. μάρτυς has begun its transition from "witness" to "martyr". Cf. Acts 22: 20.

8. Cf. Rev. 1: 2, where John "bore witness to the word of God and to the testimony of Jesus Christ".

(Rev. 1: 1, 9). When the followers of Jesus are assaulted by the dragon and his agents, they "conquered him by the blood of the Lamb and by the word of their testimony, for they loved not their lives even unto death" (Rev. 12: 11). No doubt their Lord was bearing *his* testimony in theirs, and suffering in them, but it is through their own testimony that they conquer, and their own testimony is that which they bear to Jesus and his redeeming power. It is this testimony, John is assured, that is the very substance of the Spirit of prophecy.

In the New English Bible the statement that "the testimony of Jesus is the Spirit of prophecy" is paraphrased : "those who bear testimony to Jesus are inspired like the prophets" (with the marginal alternative, "testimony to Jesus is the spirit that inspires prophets"). Some support for this interpretation may be found in the parallel statements made by the interpreting angel in protest against John's instinctive act of homage to him: "I am a fellow-servant with you and your brethren who hold the testimony of Jesus" (Rev. 19: 10) and "I am a fellow-servant with you and your brethren the prophets" (Rev. 22: 9). "Your brethren who hold the testimony of Jesus" are practically equated with "your brethren the prophets". In measure it is certainly true that the Spirit who bore (and still bears) his testimony through the prophets is the Spirit who enabled the confessors and martyrs of John's day and later days to witness a good confession. "When they bring you to trial and deliver you up", says Jesus in the Olivet discourse, "do not be anxious beforehand what you are to say; but say whatever is given you in that hour, for it is not you who speak, but the Holy Spirit" (Mark 13: 11; cf. Matt. 10: 19 f.).[9]

The fact that the Holy Spirit speaks through the confessors

---

9. Cf. the parallel in Luke 21: 15, quoted below (p. 111).

means that, to the extent at least to which they bear their testimony at his prompting, they are prophets. They are not prophets in the more regular sense in which John and others endowed with the gift of prophecy in the church are prophets, but the difference is one of degree, not of kind.[10]

Formal quotations from the Old Testament are rare in the Apocalypse, yet there is no book of the New Testament more full of Old Testament echoes. Without endorsing Austin Farrer's interpretation of the book, one can acknowledge the aptness of the title of one of his studies in it as a description of its contents: *A Rebirth of Images*.[11] To call the book an apocalyptic work, as is commonly done, is not very illuminating; it is in effect to say that it belongs to the literary *genre* which is called after it. Other apocalypses came to be so called because they partake of the general literary character of *the* Apocalypse – "the revelation (or unveiling) of Jesus Christ" as it proclaims itself to be in its opening sentence, in the sense that it unfolds the contents of the sealed scroll which he is seen receiving from God in the vision of the fifth chapter.

Jesus Christ, having received it in his rôle as the Lamb once slain, communicates its substance by his angel to his servant John on Patmos, that he in turn may impart it to the seven churches in Asia. John himself calls the book a "prophecy" (Rev. 1: 3; 22: 18); it is inspired, that is to say, by the same Spirit of prophecy as spoke through the prophets in earlier days, and the burden of the Spirit's ministry is still the testimony of Jesus – with this difference, that the one to whom the Spirit bore witness in advance through the earlier prophets has come to earth and died and risen again, and is now seated alongside his Father on the throne of glory,

10. Cf. E. Schweizer: "It seems to me ... that acc. to 19: 10 all members of the community (at least potentially ...) are prophets" (*TDNT* vi, p. 449).
11. Westminster: Dacre Press, 1949.

pending the hour of his final manifestation. When the Spirit speaks to the churches, he conveys the testimony of "Jesus Christ, the faithful witness", and reminds them of their call to be faithful witnesses in their turn.

The promise and hope proclaimed by the Old Testament prophets find fresh expression in the Revelation, but here, as emphatically as anywhere in the New Testament, it is made clear that their fulfilment is bound up with the redemptive achievement of Jesus. When, with the blowing of the seventh trumpet, it is announced that "the kingdom of the world has become the kingdom of our Lord and of his anointed, and he shall reign for ever and ever" (Rev. 11: 15), the elders' song of praise which greets the announcement confirms that the language of the second psalm is being echoed. This is the final defeat of all attempted rebellions "against the LORD and his anointed" (Psalm 2: 2); but in the wider context of the Revelation the designation, "his anointed", has a depth of meaning not hinted at by the psalmist. For now the Lord's anointed is seen to be the Lamb, who does not wait passively for hostile forces to be subdued beneath his feet but himself wages the warfare and wins the victory. John's vision of the adoration of the Lamb shows that the unfolding and consummation of the divine purpose are dependent on the sacrifice of the cross. Because of this, the Lamb – once slaughtered and now exalted – is worthy to share the worship ascribed to the Almighty: "To him who sits upon the throne and to the Lamb be blessing and honour and glory and might for ever and ever!" (Rev. 5: 13).

Fittingly, then, the initial salutation of grace and peace is pronounced not only from the eternal God and from the seven spirits who are before his throne (traditionally explained as the Spirit of God in his sevenfold plenitude of grace)[12] but also "from Jesus Christ the faithful witness, the

12. Cf. F. F. Bruce, "The Spirit in the Apocalypse", in *Christ and Spirit in the New*

firstborn from the dead and the ruler of kings on earth" (Rev. 1: 4 f.). The wording is drawn from Psalm 89: the description of the Davidic king as "the firstborn, the highest of the kings of the earth" (verse 27) is naturally applicable to the Christian Messiah, but the enigmatic "faithful witness" in the skies (verse 37) is also transferred from its original reference and applied to him.[13]

In the execution of judgment the Lamb plays an essential part (like the Son in John 5: 22 f., 27): the cataclysm unleashed by the breaking of the sixth seal forces great and small alike to call to the mountains and rocks to fall on them and hide them "from the face of him who is seated on the throne and from the wrath of the Lamb" (Rev. 6: 16) – the last expression being a striking one indeed, conveying in paradoxical terms the apostolic proclamation that Jesus is "the one ordained by God to be judge of the living and the dead" (Acts 10: 42; cf. 17: 31; Rom. 2: 16).[14]

More congenially, the blessings of the gospel are symbolized by the river of life "flowing from the throne of God and of the Lamb" – the throne established in the heart of the beloved community, the new Jerusalem, as the centre and source of peace and light (Rev. 22: 1–5).[15] The testimony of Jesus borne by the Spirit of prophecy points to him as the one in whom (to quote Pauline language) "all the promises of God find their Yes" (2 Cor. 1: 20).

## 3. The Spirit of prophecy

The expression "the Spirit of prophecy" is current in

---

*Testament: Studies in honour of C. F. D. Moule*, ed. B. Lindars and S. S. Smalley (Cambridge, 1973), pp. 333 ff.

13. It is uncertain whether the witness in the skies is the moon (as the parallelism would suggest) or the rainbow (as in Gen. 9: 12–17).

14. Cf. A. T. Hanson, *The Wrath of the Lamb* (London, 1957).

15. See p. 113.

post-biblical Judaism: it is used, for example, in a Targumic circumlocution for the Spirit of Yahweh which comes upon this or that prophet. Thus the Targum of Jonathan renders the opening words of Isa. 61: 1 as "The Spirit of prophecy from before the Lord God is upon me". The thought expresed in Rev. 19: 10 is not dissimilar to that already quoted from 1 Pet. 1: 11 where "the Spirit of Christ" is said to have borne advance testimony in the Old Testament prophets.[16] There too Jesus is the theme of the witness borne by the prophetic Spirit; the prophets did not know who the person or what the time would be, but at last the secret is out: the person is Jesus; the time is now.

In Rev. 19: 10, however, it is through *Christian* prophets that the Spirit of prophecy bears witness. What the prophets of pre-Christian days foretold is proclaimed as an accomplished fact by the prophets of the new age, among whom John occupies a leading place.

When the word "prophets" is used generally in the Apocalypse, Old Testament prophets may be included, but New Testament prophets are in the forefront. "Saints and apostles and prophets" are called upon to rejoice over the downfall of great Babylon because "in her was found the blood of prophets and of saints, and of all who have been slain on earth" (Rev. 18: 20, 24). The comprehensive terms of the last clause may imply that from great Babylon, as from the generation of Jesus' day in Luke 11: 50 f., reparation should be required for "the blood of all the prophets shed from the foundation of the world".[17] But first and foremost the saints and prophets directly killed by great Babylon are in view, for when John sees great Babylon in the guise of the scarlet woman, she is "drunk with the blood

16. See p. 98.
17. In Matt. 23: 35 "the blood of all the prophets" is generalized to "all the righteous blood shed on earth".

of the saints and the blood of the witnesses of Jesus" (Rev. 17: 6).

The burden of the prophecy entrusted to John and his fellow-prophets, then, is "the testimony of Jesus"; it is specifically the Spirit of prophecy who bears the testimony in them. Thus the ministry of the two witnesses of Rev. 11: 3 ff. is statedly a *prophetic* ministry (verses 3, 6); the *Spirit* of prophecy is not explicitly mentioned, but is certainly to be inferred, in the record of their testimony.[18] (The "breath of life" from God which enters them three and a half days after their martyrdom is the creative "breath of life" first mentioned in Gen. 2: 7 and not the prophetic Spirit.) Features of their ministry are purposely included so as to place them in the succession of Moses and Elijah, and in verse 4 their function is symbolized in terms of the two olive trees and two pipes conveying oil to the golden lampstand in Zech. 4: 12, in one of Zechariah's visions which supplied the author of the Apocalypse with further symbolism.[19]

In addition to "the Spirit of prophecy", we have in Rev. 22: 6 a reference to "the spirits of the prophets" ("the God of the spirits of the prophets", John is told, "has sent his angel to show his servants what must soon take place"). The plural expression denotes not the one Spirit of prophecy but rather the spirits of the individual prophets, as in 1 Cor. 14: 32, where it appears in the anarthrous form: "spirits of prophets are subject to prophets". There may be an echo in Rev. 22: 6 of the Old Testament phrase, "God of the spirits of all flesh"

18. The adverb πνευματικῶς in the vision of the two witnesses is used of the interpretation of Jerusalem, "where their Lord was crucified", as "the great city which is *spiritually* called Sodom and Egypt" (Rev. 11: 8). Whereas the adverb is commonly rendered "allegorically" (so RSV; cf. NEB "in allegory"), E. Schweizer takes it to mean "in prophetic rather than ordinary speech" (*TDNT* vi, p. 449 with n. 819).

19. Thus the Lamb's "seven eyes, which are the seven spirits of God sent out into all the earth" (Rev. 5: 6) have their background in Zech. 4: 2, 10b.

(Num. 16: 22; 27: 16); he who creates and controls all human spirits has a special concern for "the spirits of the prophets" who are his spokesmen on earth.

When the Spirit of prophecy comes upon him, John speaks of himself as being, or becoming, "in Spirit". So his inaugural vision is introduced with the words (literally translated), "I became in Spirit on the Lord's day" (Rev. 1: 10); his second vision, in which he was rapt to heaven, is similarly introduced with "immediately I became in Spirit" (Rev. 4: 2); and for two later visions – that of the scarlet woman and that of the bride of the Lamb – he is carried away "in Spirit" by an angel to an appropriate vantage-point (Rev. 17: 3; 21: 10). In these last two passages especially, his language is strongly reminiscent of Ezekiel's, although Ezekiel uses other expressions than "in Spirit". Ezekiel's nearest approach to this phraseology is in Ezek. 37: 1, "the hand of Yahweh was upon me and carried me out in the Spirit of Yahweh". Elsewhere he says "the Spirit lifted me up, and took me away" (Ezek. 3: 14; cf. 8: 3, etc.). The Spirit performs for Ezekiel the service performed for John by one of the seven angels who stand before the heavenly throne, but the same type of ecstasy is described under the variant terminology.

### 4. *What the Spirit says to the churches*

The exhortation at the end of each of the letters to the seven churches (preceding the promise to the overcomer in the first three, following it in the last four), "He who has an ear, let him hear what the Spirit says to the churches",[20] should give the reader pause. For each of these letters is sent in the name of the exalted Christ, who is introduced by one designation or another, largely drawn from John's descrip-

20. Rev. 2: 7a, 11a, 17a, 29; 3: 6, 13, 22.

tion of him in his inaugural vision. The letter to the Ephesian church, for instance (Rev. 2: 1–7), begins with "The words of him who holds the seven stars in his right hand (cf. 1: 16), who walks among the seven golden lampstands" (cf. 1: 13), but towards the end comes the exhortation to the attentive hearer to pay heed to what *the Spirit* says (2: 7a). The conclusion is plain: it is not that the Spirit is completely identical with the exalted Lord,[21] but that the exalted Lord speaks to the churches by the Spirit – and the Spirit here can scarcely be other than the Spirit of prophecy. The words which John writes to the churches by the Lord's command he writes as a prophet.

Nor is it only in these letters that he speaks by the Spirit of prophecy in the name of the exalted Lord. One prophetic utterance thus made in his name is of special interest. When John sees the kings of the earth mustering for the battle of Har-Magedon "on the great day of God the Almighty", a voice declares: "Lo, I am coming like a thief! Blessed is he who is awake, keeping his garments that he may not go naked and be seen exposed!" (Rev. 16: 15).[22] The voice is self-evidently that of the exalted Lord, but it echoes a logion ascribed in the Gospels to the earthly Jesus, in a life-setting which is perfectly appropriate. The thief simile, which has already been used by the exalted Lord in the letter to the church of Sardis as an incentive to stay awake (Rev. 3: 3), is used by the historical Jesus in a Synoptic utterance (Matt. 24: 43//Luke 12: 39), where the day of visitation comes unexpectedly as a thief.[23] We may infer that a prophetic utterance in the name of Jesus was liable to take up an

---

21. As E. Schweizer suggests (*TDNT* vi, p. 449).

22. R. H. Charles (*The Revelation of St. John*, ii (Edinburgh, 1920), p. 49) maintains that Rev. 16: 15 is an intrusion here, either from 3: 13 (so J. Moffatt) or from before 3: 18 (so Th. de Bèze).

23. Cf. also 1 Thess. 5:2; 2 Pet. 3: 10.

authentic *verbum Christi* and adapt or point it to the current situation, as here the logion is elaborated by the blessing pronounced on the man who is alert and ready dressed, so that when the alarm is sounded he has no need to take to flight naked, like the man "who is stout of heart among the mighty" in Amos 2: 16.

This is a more probable account of the relation between the prophetic office in the early church and the gospel tradition than the view that inspired utterances in the name of the risen Christ were read back into the ministry of the earthly Jesus. Indeed, much of the contents of the Apocalypse as such could be understood as an expansion of the Olivet discourse of Mark 13: 5 ff. (and parallels). The Olivet discourse in the gospel tradition, however, is introduced by a conversation between Jesus and the disciples (verses 1–4) which has as its most natural life-setting that which Mark gives it.

We might think similarly of the revelation about the destiny of the faithful departed in 1 Thess. 4: 15 ff., which Paul communicates "by the word of the Lord"; while it is possible that he refers to a prophetic utterance in the Lord's name, it is equally possible (and rather more probable) that he is citing or applying a saying which he had "received" by tradition. The prophetic *genre* has its own characteristics, which cannot be transferred without more ado to other literary *genres*. Paul, like the seer of Patmos, sends letters to various churches, and occasionally claims as authority for what he writes the mind of the Spirit or the commandment of the Lord,[24] but he sends his letters in his own name (quite emphatically so), not in the name of the Lord.

A closer parallel to the Apocalypse is presented by the *Odes of Solomon* which, while they are not assigned to the apocalyp-

24. Cf. 1 Cor. 2: 16b; 7: 40b; 14: 37.

tic *genre*, breathe the spirit of prophecy, especially where Christ himself is the speaker. He says, for example, "I rose up and was with them, and speak by their mouths" (Ode 42: 6).[25] But this apparently refers not to prophets in particular but to those who love him in general (Ode 42: 4), and especially in the context of persecution, so that it is to the same effect as the passage in the Lukan edition of the Olivet discourse where Jesus tells his disciples that when they are brought to trial for their faith, "I will give you a mouth and wisdom" (Luke 21: 15).[26]

## 5. The responsive Spirit

The Spirit in the prophets is immediately responsive to the will of heaven.[27] So, when John is directed by a heavenly voice to write, "Blessed are the dead who die in the Lord henceforth" (Rev. 14: 13), the Spirit adds his Amen: "Blessed indeed, . . . that they may rest from their labours, for their deeds accompany them!"[28] For apostates and confessors alike it is true that "their deeds accompany them" beyond the grave, but whereas for the former this means tribulation, for the latter it means rest (cf. 2 Thess. 1: 6 f.). The significance and construction of "henceforth" are debatable: the "saints, those who keep the commandments

25. R. Bultmann cites this passage among others in the *Odes of Solomon* which (he says) provide clear examples of the ascription to the historical Jesus in the gospel tradition of inspired utterances delivered in his name (*The History of the Synoptic Tradition*, E. T. [Oxford, 1963], pp. 127 f., n. 1).

26. Here "I" (Christ himself) corresponds to "the Holy Spirit" in the parallel Mark 13: 11 (cf. Matt. 10. 20). Luke's own illustration of the fulfilment of this promise may be recognized in his account of Stephen: "they could not withstand the wisdom and the Spirit with which he spoke" (Acts 6: 10).

27. Cf. the responses made by the angel of the waters (Rev. 16: 5) and by the altar (16: 7).

28. Cf. *Pirqê Abot* 6: 9 ("in the hour of man's departure neither silver nor gold nor precious stones accompany him, but only Torah and good works").

of God and the faith of Jesus" (Rev. 14: 12) may be given this beatitude as an incentive to endure from now on. Yet, if they suffered martyrdom, their future lot was never other than blessed. Perhaps "henceforth" means "after they have suffered martyrdom" or, as has been suggested, the Greek term should be accented differently and rendered not "henceforth" but "verily".[29]

Again, when "the Spirit and the Bride say 'Come' " (Rev. 22: 17a), this is the response to the Lord's announcement in verse 12: "Behold, I am coming quickly". It may be that "the Spirit and the Bride", in H. B. Swete's words, is an expression "practically equivalent to 'the Prophets and the Saints'."[30] If so, the Spirit of prophecy in the prophets receives a confirming echo from the Spirit of response in the saints, but these are not two Spirits, but two rôles of the one Spirit. The Spirit who has spoken by the prophets is the Spirit who illuminates the saints, enabling them to acknowledge the prophetic witness and to make it their own.

The words immediately following, "And let him who hears say, 'Come' " (Rev. 22: 17b), constitute a call to those who are listening to the reading of the Apocalypse in the churches (cf. Rev. 1:3) to interpose at this point with their own "Come!" We cannot dissociate this passage from the use of the invocation *Maranatha* in the early church. In the eucharistic setting in which the invocation appears in the *Didache* (10: 6), it is preceded by the call:

> If anyone is holy, let him come;
> if anyone is not, let him repent.

29. Reading ἀπαρτί for ἀπ' ἄρτι, with A. Debrunner in *Coniectanea Neotestamentica* 11 (1947), p. 184, quoted with approval by A. Oepke, *TDNT* v, p. 867, n. 50 (*s.v. παρουσία*). If ἀπ' ἄρτι be read, it is construed more naturally with ἀποθνῄσκοντες ("dying") than with μακάριοι ("blessed").

30. H. B. Swete, *The Apocalypse of St. John* (London, 1906), p. 306 (he compares Rev. 16: 6; 18: 24).

The invitation "let him come" presents a marked affinity to the words in the Apocalypse which follow the call to the hearer: "And let him who is thirsty come, let him who desires take the water of life without price" (cf. Isa. 55: 1) – take it from the Alpha and Omega who, as Rev. 21: 6 declares, has the authority and the will to grant it.

The water of life is drawn from the river of Rev. 22: 1 f., which flows through the New Jerusalem. The imagery is derived from the life-giving river of Ezek. 47:1 ff. and similar Old Testament oracles, but when we consider that in the New Testament the figure of the water of life appears only in the Fourth Gospel and the Apocalypse, we are bound to think (as we have thought already) of the "rivers of living water" promised by Jesus in John 7: 37 ff.[31] The evangelist explains this living water as a figure of the Spirit, and similarly (although the seer does not himself make the identification explicitly) the water to be had without price in Rev. 21: 6b and 22: 17b may be identified with the Spirit – but if so, it is as the Spirit of life rather than as the Spirit of prophecy that he is now in view, together with the blessings of the gospel which he imparts.

To revert to the invitation, whereas the *Didache* holds out the hope of repentance to one who is not holy, the situation in the Apocalypse is more urgent, and space for repentance is practically excluded: "Let the evildoer still do evil, . . . and the holy still be holy" (Rev. 22: 11).

It is of relevance here to recall that in 1 Cor. 16: 22 (its earliest recorded occurrence) *Maranatha* follows immediately upon the anathema pronounced on any one who "has no love for the Lord", while in Rev. 22: 20 the invocation "Amen: come, Lord Jesus!" is preceded by the solemn curse of verses 18 f. on any one who tampers with "the words of the book of

31. See pp. 46 f.

this prophecy". The curse is introduced with "I testify" and followed by the words, "He who testifies to these things says, 'Surely I am coming quickly'."[32]

Probably the invitation to the seeker and the ban on the reprobate are both associated with the invocation "Come!" The nearness of the Lord, which is a comfort to believers, means judgment for the impenitent. In Rev. 21: 7 f. the overcomer's heritage of divine sonship is proclaimed in the same breath as the sentence to the "second death" on those who in speech or conduct have forsworn the faith.

When the Lord manifests his real presence in the holy supper, the humble are encouraged to draw near and partake; the self-centred and hard-hearted are warned off lest they eat and drink judgment to themselves. The Lord's coming in the Apocalypse is more than his eucharistic presence, but it is anticipated in his eucharistic presence, as the separation of the righteous from the unrighteous at his coming is anticipated by the two-way fencing of the holy table. The most solemn act of the church's worship could thus have provided an appropriate occasion for the public reading of the Apocalypse, and such an occasion may have been in the seer's mind as he recorded the concluding sentences of his vision. The "testimony of Jesus" which is brought home to faithful communicants in the Lord's Supper is identical with the testimony borne to him by the Spirit of prophecy and provides a way for the indwelling Spirit to seal in their hearts the witness of Scripture.

32. Cf. C. F. D. Moule, "A Reconsideration of the Context of *Maranatha*", *NTS* 6 (1959–60), pp. 307 ff.

INDEXES

# INDEX OF NAMES AND SUBJECTS

# INDEX OF BIBLICAL REFERENCES

## OLD TESTAMENT